THE ASIAN WORLD, 600–1500

BONNIE G. SMITH
GENERAL EDITOR

THE ASIAN WORLD, 600–1500

Roger V. Des Forges & John S. Major

OXFORD
UNIVERSITY PRESS

For Alexa Des Forges Poremba—R. V. D.
For Steve Major—J. S. M.

OXFORD
UNIVERSITY PRESS

Oxford University Press, Inc., publishes works that further
Oxford University's objective of excellence
in research, scholarship, and education.

Oxford New York
Auckland Cape Town Dar es Salaam Hong Kong Karachi
Kuala Lumpur Madrid Melbourne Mexico City Nairobi
New Delhi Shanghai Taipei Toronto

With offices in
Argentina Austria Brazil Chile Czech Republic France Greece
Guatemala Hungary Italy Japan Poland Portugal Singapore
South Korea Switzerland Thailand Turkey Ukraine Vietnam

Published by Oxford University Press, Inc.
198 Madison Avenue, New York, New York 10016
www.oup.com

Oxford is a registered trademark of Oxford University Press

Design: Stephanie Blumenthal and Alexis Siroc
Cover design and logo: Nora Wertz

Library of Congress Cataloging-in-Publication Data

Des Forges, Roger V.
The Asian world, 600–1500 / Roger Des Forges, John S. Major.
p. cm. — (Medieval & early modern world)
ISBN-13: 978-019-517843-2 — 978-019-522266-1 (Calif. ed.) — 978-019-522157-2 (set)
ISBN-10: 0-19-517843-2 — 0-19-522266-0 (Calif. ed.) 0-19-522157-5 (set)

1. Asia—History. I. Major, John S. II. Title. III. Medieval and early modern world
DS33.5.D47 2005
950'.1—dc22
2004021415

9 8 7 6 5 4 3 2 1

Printed in the United States on acid-free paper.

On the cover: A whistling terracotta actor from the Yuan dynasty in China.
Frontispiece: A painting of three noblemen, from the Buddhist cave temples at Bezeklik, China.

BONNIE G. SMITH

GENERAL EDITOR

DIANE L. BROOKS, Ed. D.

EDUCATION CONSULTANT

The European World, 400–1450
Barbara A. Hanawalt

The African and Middle Eastern World, 600–1500
Randall L. Pouwels

The Asian World, 600–1500
Roger V. Des Forges and John S. Major

An Age of Empires, 1200–1750
Marjorie Wall Bingham

An Age of Voyages, 1350–1600
Merry E. Wiesner-Hanks

An Age of Science and Revolutions, 1600–1800
Toby E. Huff

**The Medieval and Early Modern World:
Primary Sources & Reference Volume**
Donald R. Kelley and Bonnie G. Smith

CONTENTS

A ❝ marks a primary source—a piece of writing that speaks to us from the past.

CAST OF CHARACTERS   9

MAP OF THE ASIAN WORLD, 600–1500   14

INTRODUCTION: A Dinner Party in Tang China   16

Chapter 1   TWO TEACHERS: Buddha, Kongzi, and Early India and China   20
MASTER KONG • KINGS AND SAINTS • GOT SILK?
❝ Verses from the Lotus Sutra, about 100 BCE   24

Chapter 2   CHINA UNITED, AGAIN: The Sui and Tang Dynasties   31
SUI SUCCEEDS, AT FIRST • THE TANG TAKES UP THE TASK • A CROWING HEN
❝ Bai Juyi, "Song of Unending Sorrow," about 820 CE   41

Chapter 3   RAJAS AND SULTANS: The Struggle for India   43
KING HARSHA • ISLAM AND INDIA •
SOUTH AND NORTH
❝ Kalidasa, "The Birth of the War God,"
about 400 CE   50

Chapter 4   TRADE IF BY LAND AND TRADE IF BY SEA:
Merchants, Religion, and Ideas   55
CAMELS AND SILK • A WATERY ROAD •
HINDU AND BUDDHIST KINGDOMS
❝ Bureau of History, *History of the Tang Dynasty*, mid-10th century CE   65

Chapter 5   BONES AND BUDDHISTS: Early Korea and Japan   66
PRINCE SHOTOKU CHANGES THE RULES •
A GOLDEN AGE FOR THE UPPER CRUST
❝ Murasaki Shikibu, *The Tale of Genji*,
about 1010 CE   76

Chapter 6 **HORSEMEN AND GENTLEMEN: The Song Dynasty in China** **78**
THIS TEST *REALLY* COUNTS • SHIPS, ROCKETS, AND PHILOSOPHERS •
BIG CITIES AND SMALL FEET
‟ Su Shi, "Essay on the Bamboo Paintings of Wen Tong," about 1070 CE 82

Chapter 7 **KHANS AND CONQUEST: The Mongol Empire** **91**
IT TAKES A TRIBE • RESISTANCE IS FUTILE • HERE COME THE TAXMEN
‟ Rashid al-Din, *The Complete Collection of Histories*, about 1307 CE 101

Chapter 8 **SULTANS, SLAVES, AND SOUTHERNERS: The Sultanate
of Delhi in India** **102**
ONE WOMAN WARRIOR AND TWO AMBITIOUS SULTANS •
THE NORTH ATTACKS, THE SOUTH RESISTS
‟ Abu 'Abdallah Ibn Battuta, *Travels*, 1347 CE 109

Chapter 9 **KHAN AND EMPEROR: The Yuan Dynasty in China** **113**
BACK TO A SIMPLER LIFE • KHUBILAI BITES OFF MORE
THAN HE CAN CHEW
‟ Marco Polo, *Travels*, 1298 CE 122

Chapter 10 **WARRIORS RULE: Kamakura and Ashikaga Japan** **124**
BE TRUE TO YOUR SCHOOL • FOR WHOM
THE WIND BLOWS • ZEN ARTS
‟ Yoshida Kenko, *Essays in Idleness*,
about 1350 CE 130

Chapter 11   **FRESH DAWN: Koryo and Early Choson Korea**   **136**
MAKING FRIENDS WITH THE MING • A GREAT KING
AND HIS GRAND INVENTIONS
Choson Officials, *History of the Koryo Dynasty*,
1451 CE   142

Chapter 12   **RISE AND SHINE: Rulers and Treasure Ships in
Ming China**   **148**
TAIZU TAKES COMMAND • THE VOYAGES OF THE
TREASURE FLEETS
Feng Menglong, "The God of the Archery Target Helps Win
the War," from *The Expanded Treasury of Laughs*, 1574–1645 CE   160

GLOSSARY   **161**

TIMELINE   **164**

FURTHER READING   **167**

WEBSITES   **170**

INDEX   **171**

TEXT AND PICTURE CREDITS   **174**

CAST OF CHARACTERS

Abu 'Abdallah ibn Battuta, *see* Ibn Battuta

Airlangga (EYE-er-LANG-ga), ruled 1016–1045 • Hindu king of an island state in Southeast Asian

Ala-ud-din Khalji (ah-lah-ood-deen CALL-jee), about 1270–1316 • Sultan of Delhi, India

An Lushan (ahn loo-shahn), d. 757 • Chinese Tang dynasty general who started rebellion leading to civil war

Ashoka (uh-SHOK-uh), ruled about 272–232 BCE • King of the Maurya dynasty in India

Ashikaga (ah-shee-KAH-gah) • Dynasty of shoguns of Japan that lasted from 1336 to 1573, founded by Ashikaga Takauji

Ashikaga Takauji (ah-she-KAH-gah tah-kah-OO-jee), 1305–1358 • Founder of Ashikaga shogunate

Bai Juyi (buy joo-ee) also called Bo (boh) Juyi, 771–846 • Chinese Tang dynasty poet

Bhoj (BOE-ja), ruled 1018–1055 • Philosopher-king of Paramara, India

Buddha, *see* Gautama, Siddartha

Choson (CHOH-sohn), Korean dynasty that lasted from 1392 to 1910, founded by Yi Songgye

Confucius, *see* Kong Zhongni

Du Fu (doo foo) 712–770 • Chinese Tang dynasty poet

Fan Kuan (fahn kwahn), late 11th–early 12th centuries • Song dynasty landscape painter

Fujiwara Michinaga (foo-jee-wah-rah mee-chee-nah-gah), 966–1027 • Head of powerful Japanese aristocratic family

Gautama, Siddartha (GOW-tum-uh, si-DAHR-thuh), d. 420–350 BCE • The Buddha ("Enlightened One"); founder of Buddhism

Genghis Khan (JENG-hiz kahn), about 1160–1227 • Mongol conqueror; birth name **Temujin** (teh-moo-jin)

Godaigo (go-DIE-go), ruled 1318–1339 • Japanese emperor who tried to restore power to the throne

Guo Shoujing (gwoh show-jing), 1231–1314 • Chinese mathematician, astronomer, and engineer; adviser to Khubilai Khan

Han (hahn) • Chinese dynasty from 206 BCE to 220 CE

Harsha Vardhana (HAR-sha var-DAHN-ha), about 600–647 • North Indian ruler

Ho'elun (HOH eh-luhn), 12th century • Mother of Genghis Khan

Huang Chao (hwong chow), d. 884 • Leader of rebellion against China's Tang dynasty

Ibn Battuta (IB-en bah-TOO-tah), 1307–1377 • Arab traveler and writer; full name Abu 'Abdallah ibn Battuta

Ibn Sina (IB-en SEE-nah), 980–1037 • Islamic scientist and philosopher known in medieval Europe as Avicenna (AH-vih-SEN-uh)

Jin • Jurchen dynasty that ruled northern China from 1115 to 1234

Jochi (JOH-chee), about 1180–1227 • Eldest son of Genghis Khan

Kabir (kah-BEER), about 1440–1518 • Indian mystic and poet

Kafur Malik (kah-FOOR mah-lick), late 13th–early 14th centuries • Slave and general for Sultan Ala-ud-din

Khubilai Khan (KOO-buh-lie kahn), 1215–1294 • Grandson of Genghis Khan, great khan from 1260 to 1294; founded Yuan dynasty of China

Kim Wonjong (kim wohn-johng), ruled 514–540 • King of Silla, Korea

Kong Zhongni (koong joong-nee) or Kongzi (KOONG-dzuh), 551–479 BCE • Chinese philosopher and teacher known in West as Confucius

Koryo (KOH-ryuh) • Korean dynasty from 936 to 1392; founded by Wang Kon

Kumarajiva (koo-mar-ah-JEE-vah), active 385–419 • Central Asian monk; important translator of Buddhist scriptures into Chinese

Laozi (laow-dzuh) • Legendary founder of Daoism; traditionally believed to have lived in the sixth century BCE

Li Bai (lee buy) also Li Bo (lee boh), 701–762 • Chinese Tang dynasty poet

Li Qingzhao (lee ching-jao), about 1084–1151 • Song dynasty woman poet

Li Shimin, see Tang Taizong

Li Yuan (lee yooann), 566–635 • Founder and first emperor of China's Tang dynasty

Liao (lyaow) • Khitan dynasty that ruled northern China from 907 to 1125; founded by Yelü Abaoji.

Liu Bingzhong (lyoh bing-joong), 1216–1274 • Chinese scholar and adviser to Khubilai Khan

Mahadeviyakka (MA-ha-DEV-ee-YAK-ka), about 630–660 • Indian woman religious poet

Mahavira (MA-ha-VEE-ra), about 6th–5th centuries BCE • Founder of Jainism

Mahmud (ma-MOOD) of Gazni (GAHZ-nee), 971–1030 • Muslim ruler of Afghanistan who invaded India

Minamoto Yoritomo (mi-nah-MOH-toe yo-ree-TOE-mo), 1147–1199 • Founder of Kamakura shogunate

Minamoto Yoshitsune (mi-nah-MOH-toe yo-she-TSOO-neh), 1159–1189 • Brother of Yoritomo; persecuted by Yoritomo and committed suicide

Ming • Chinese dynasty from 1368 to 1644; founded by Zhu Yuanzhang

Ming Taizu, see Zhu Yuanzhang

Mongke (MUNG-kay), about 1205–1259 • Grandson of Genghis Khan; Great Khan from 1251 to 1259

Muhammad (mu-HAM-mahd), about 570–632 • Prophet and founder of Islam

Muhammad bin Tughluq (mu-HAM-mahd bin TOOG-luck), 14th century • Sultan of Delhi, India

Muhammad Ghori (mu-HAM-mahd GORE-ee), about 1150–1206 • Persian ruler who conquered northern India

Muhammad ibn Qasim (mu-HAM-mahd ib-in KASS-im), about 695–715 • Arab prince who conquered Indian province of Sind

Munjong (MUHN-johng), ruled 1450–1452 • Fourth king of Korea's Choson dynasty; sponsored historical scholarship

Murasaki Shikibu (moo-rah-sah-kee shee-kee-boo), about 976–1015 • Japanese woman author of The Tale of Genji

Muso Soseki (moo-SOH soh-seh-kee), 1275–1351 • Japanese Zen master

Nichiren (nee-chee-ren), 1222–1282 • Founder of militant Lotus Sutra sect of Japanese Buddhism

Ogodei (OH-go-day), about 1185–1241 • Son of Genghis Khan; great khan from 1229 to 1241

Polo, Marco, 1254–1324 • Italian traveler to China

Qin (chin) • Dynasty that unified China, 221–206 BCE

Qin Shi Huangdi (chin sher hwong-dee), 258–210 BCE • First Emperor and unifier of China

Qiu Chuji (chyoh choo-jee), 1148–1227 • Chinese Daoist priest; visited Genghis Khan; author of *Journey to the West*

Qutb-ud-Din Aybak (KUTB-ood-deen AYE-bahk), 12th–13th centuries • First Sultan of Delhi, India

Rashid al-Din (Rah-SHEED ahl-DEEN), 1247–1317 • Muslim statesman and historian

Raziya (RAHZ-ee-yah), about 1200–1240 • Third Sultan of Delhi, India; only woman to be sultan

Sejong (SEH-johng), 1397–1450 • Third king of Choson dynasty; Korea's greatest king

Shinran (shin-rahn), 1173–1262 • Influential Japanese Buddhist priest of Pure Land school

Shotoku, Prince (show-toe-koo), 574–622 • Japanese co-ruler with Queen Suiko; wrote 17-article constitution

Sondok (sohn-duck), ruled 632–647 • Queen of kingdom of Silla, Korea

Song (suhng) • Chinese dynasty founded by Zhao Kuangyin; Northern Song lasts from 960 to 1127 CE; Southern Song lasts from 1127 to 1260 CE

Song Taizu, *see* Zhao Kuangyin

Su Shi (soo sher) also called Su Dongpo (soo doong-paw), 1037–1101 • Song dynasty poet and critic

Sui (sway) • Chinese dynasty from 589 to 618 CE; founded by Yang Jian

Sui Wendi (sway one-dee), 541–604 • Chinese emperor and founder of Sui dynasty; personal name Yang Jian (yahng jen)

Sui Yangdi (sway yahng-dee), 569–618 • Chinese emperor; second (and last) ruler of Sui dynasty

T'aejo, King, *see* Yi Songgye

Tang (tahng) • Chinese dynasty from 618 to 907 CE; founded by Li Yuan

Tang Taizong (tahng tie-dzoong), ruled 626–648 • Second emperor of China's Tang dynasty; personal name Li Shimin (lee sher-min)

Tang Xuanzong (tahng syuan-dzoong), ruled 713–756 • Chinese emperor during Tang dynasty; had disastrous affair with concubine Yang Guifei

Temujin, *see* Genghis Khan

Timur Leng (TEE-mur lung), 1336–1405 • Central Asian conqueror known in Europe as Tamerlane

Vijayanagara (Vee-JAI-ah-nah-GAH-rah) • Dynasty in southern India from 1336 to 1565; founded by brothers Harihara and Bukka Sangama

Wang Kon (wong kun), ruled 918–943 • Founder of Koryo dynasty, Korea

Wang Wei (wong way), 699–761 • Chinese Buddhist poet and painter

Wonjong (wun jahng), ruled 1259–1274 • Korean king of Koryo dynasty; established close relations with Mongols

Wu (woo), **Emperor,** ruled 140–87 BCE • Began trade on the Silk Road

Wu Zhao (woo jao), 625–706 • Imperial concubine who became China's only female emperor

Xuanzang (syuan-dzahng), 600–664 • Chinese Buddhist pilgrim to India

Yang Guifei (yahng gway-fay), d. 756 • Favorite concubine of Tang emperor Xuanzong

Yang Jian, *see* Sui Wendi

Yelü Abaoji (YEH-lew ah-BAOW-jee), ruled 907–926 • Khitan ruler; founder and first emperor of Liao dynasty

Yelü Chucai (YEH-lew CHOO-tsai), 1189–1243 • Khitan adviser to Mongol emperors

Yi Songgye (ee sohng-gyeh), 1335–1408 • General and founder of Korea's Choson dynasty; known as King T'aejo (TIE-joh)

Yongle, *see* Zhu Di

Yoshida Kenko (YOH-shee-da KEN-koh), 1283–1350 • Japanese aristocrat, poet, and monk; wrote *Essays in Idleness*

Yu Xuanji (yoo syuan-jee), 843–868 • One of China's great woman poets

Yuan (yooann) • Mongol dynasty that ruled China from 1279 to 1368; founded by Khubilai Khan

Zhao Kuangyin (jao kwong-yin), ruled 960–976 • Founder of Song dynasty; also known as Song Taizu (suhng tie-dzoo)

Zhao Mengfu (jao mung-foo), 1254–1322 • Chinese artist and scholar-official under Yuan dynasty

Zheng He (jeng huh), 1371–1433 • Eunuch admiral who led Ming "treasure fleet" voyages

Zhu Di (joo dee), 1360–1424 • Second emperor of Ming dynasty; known as Yongle (yuhng-luh); sponsored "treasure fleet" voyages

Zhu Xi (joo syee), 1130–1200 • Song dynasty scholar and philosopher

Zhu Yuanzhang (joo yooann-jahng), 1328–1398 • Founder of Ming dynasty; known as Ming Taizu (TIE-dzoo)

SOME PRONUNCIATIONS

Kamakura (kah-mah-KOO-rah)

Beijing (bay-jing)

Bukhara (boo-KAHR-ah)

Chang'an (chahng-ahn)

Dadu (dah-doo)

Delhi (DEH-lee)

Fancheng (fahn-chuhng)

Ganga (guhn-GAH) River

Ghazni (GAHZ-nee)

Guangzhou (gwahng-jo)

Hangzhou (hahng-jo)

Hanyang (hahn-yahng)

Heian-kyō (HEY-ahn-KYOH)

Huang He (hwong huh)

Irrawaddy River (ih-ruh-WUD-ee)

Kaifeng (kai-fuhng)

Lake Baikal (BUY-kahl)

Lin'an (linn-ahn)

Mekong River (MAY-kahng)

Samarkand (SA-muhr-kand)

Shangdu (shahng-doo)

Xiangyang (syahng-yahng)

Yangzi (yahng-dzuh)

THE ASIAN WORLD, 600—1500

RUSSIA

Lake
Baikal

Lake
Balkash

MONGOLIA

ASIA

amarkand

Shangdu

Dadu
(Beijing)

Huang He
(Yellow River)

KOREA

Sea of
Japan

JAPAN

Kamakura

Heian-kyō
Nara

Inland
Sea

Yalu River

Kaifeng

Himalayas

TIBET

Chang'an

Xiangyang

Fancheng

Hanyang

Lin'an
(Hangzhou)

Delhi

Ganga

River

Yangzi River

CHINA

Pacific Ocean

INDIA

Irrawaddy River

BURMA

Bay of
Bengal

Salween River

Guangzhou

Mekong River

South
China
Sea

Borneo

VIETNAM

Sumatra

Java

INTRODUCTION
A DINNER PARTY IN TANG CHINA

As the autumn evening grows dark, waitresses in the expensive restaurant hurry to light the oil lamps in the private upstairs dining room. The place is Chang'an, the capital of Tang dynasty China. The time is the 38th year of Emperor Xuanzong, or, as we would say, the year 750 CE. The party that we are imagining has been going for an hour or two already, and the guests wear the satisfied look of people who have just finished a very good meal. They have eaten fish stuffed with garlic, roasted pheasant, and other fancy dishes. In the warm lamplight they settle down for after-dinner drinks, conversation, and music that will last well into the night.

Chang'an in 750 is the largest and most culturally diverse city in the world. The borders of China stretch from the Pacific Ocean in the east to the far west along the Silk Road into Central Asia, and from Korea and Mongolia in the north to Vietnam and Burma in the south. The city's population of about 1 million people includes not only Chinese, but also Koreans and Japanese, Indians and Malays, Persians and Armenians, Tibetans, and Turks. There are Confucianists and Daoists and Buddhists, Christians and Muslims and Jews. The foreign residents are there to buy and sell goods, to teach and to study, and to enjoy the cultural richness of a great city.

The guests at the dinner party can afford an expensive evening, because China during the Tang dynasty is rich as well as big. The country's economy is based on agriculture. The flatlands of the central plain, stretching north and south of the Huang He (Yellow River), are covered in fields of wheat, millet, and soybeans. Farther south, terraced rice fields in the vast Yangzi River valley yield abundant harvests. On almost every farm in the country, there is a grove of mulberry trees; the leaves are used to feed silk-worms, which produce silk thread that the farm-women weave into cloth. Silk production is important to China's economy, and silk cloth is one of the main items in the country's international trade.

The guests at the dinner party mostly come from wealthy families that own large amounts of land and collect rent, paid in grain and silk, from the peasant farmers. Some of the guests also hold high government offices, which pay handsome salaries. To be appointed to those offices, they first had to pass difficult exams based on China's classical philosophy, literature, and history. The people at the party are rich, confident, well educated, and interested in the world around them.

The restaurant where our party is taking place is not only expensive, but very trendy as well. The waitresses wear daring outfits in the fashionable Turkish style: tight jackets over colorful silk blouses, and loose, baggy trousers. The young women are dressed as if they have just come from playing a game of polo. Older, conservative Chinese men were shocked by such clothing—"Our women are acting like foreigners' wives," one poet complained. And, they were offended by the idea of young women playing rough, masculine games such as polo. But, of course, shocking conservative older men was part of the fun.

In a detail from a long scroll painting, a woman plays the qin, a traditional Chinese stringed instrument similar to the Western zither, in the garden of the Tang imperial palace. A maid serves tea, a drink that became popular in China during the Tang dynasty.

Some of the male guests are dressed in the long, loose-sleeved robes favored by scholars and artists, and others wear military-style tunics and riding trousers. Two of the men are visiting diplomats from Korea: one of them is wearing the maroon patchwork robe of a Buddhist monk. There are women guests, too, well educated and comfortable attending a private party with their male friends. One woman poet wears the gray robes of a Buddhist nun; others are dressed in fashionable high-waisted silk dresses topped by boldly patterned silk jackets. Their hair is piled high on their heads in elaborate loops and buns, held in place with hairpins of white Burmese jade. Some wear golden hair ornaments accented with brilliant blue kingfisher feathers, imported from the southern borderlands near Vietnam. They wear make-up designed to emphasize a sweet, round-faced look, in the style of the emperor's favorite young wife, who is said to be rather plump.

Everyone at the party grows quiet as the guest of honor rises to recite some of his poems. Wang Wei is a poet and painter from a very rich and socially prominent family. Despite his wealth he has adopted a simple lifestyle and has devoted himself to Buddhism. In a quiet voice he begins: "My fishing boat sails the river. I love spring in the mountains. . . . " After reciting three or four poems he signals that his voice is tired, and the waitresses bring fresh drinks for everyone.

As Wang Wei sits down again, several young women enter the room and begin tuning their musical instruments. This is a very special treat. They are an all-female orchestra from the distant Central Asian city of Samarkand, on a performing tour of China. Their promoter has booked them to play at many private parties like this one; he expects the tour to be a great financial success. As the musicians begin to play Persian-style music on instruments that look like lutes and long-necked banjos, accompanied by flutes and drums, the guests are delighted. The fast, rhythmic music has all the guests tapping their feet. They are even more pleased when two young women, wearing silk trousers, bright blouses, red shoes, and tall hats with golden bells attached, enter the room and begin to dance.

All too soon, the musicians go on to another party, but the guests are not ready to leave yet. Someone suggests a poetry game: Wang Wei is invited to propose a first line, and each guest has to add another line within two minutes. A water clock is brought in to time the intervals, and the game begins. The Korean diplomats are pleased by this; their spoken Chinese is not perfect, but they can read and write Chinese well, and they are good at this game. Later, brushes, ink, and paper are brought in so the guests can write down the best poems as souvenirs of a delightful evening. Then the guests call their servants, who have been waiting patiently in the restaurant's courtyard throughout the evening, and everyone goes home.

This imaginary Tang dinner party reminds us that none of the cultures and nations of Asia developed in absolute isolation from the others. Asia is both huge and diverse. It includes every kind of natural and human environment: mountains and prairies, river valleys and deserts, farmlands and forests, cities and villages. Asia is composed of many different cultures and nations. Its peoples are of many ethnic groups and speak many languages. Yet objects and ideas—everything from cotton and silk cloth, to styles of music and art, to religious beliefs—have traveled among the different regions, countries, and cultures of Asia, each influencing the other. Not only in eighth-century China but in many times and places in Asian history, cultures have influenced one another and people have been open to new ideas and ways of doing things.

On the one hand, the cultures and countries of Asia, such as India, China, and Japan, have had histories that are quite different from each other. On the other hand, the contact among these cultures over the course of history has constantly changed them, often in surprising ways. Such contact sometimes led to war and conquest, but also, sometimes stimulated leaders to establish large, centralized states that brought some peace and order to many people over long periods of time.

During the Tang dynasty, China was open to new forms of art and culture imported from foreign lands. Traders, Buddhist monks, and other travelers introduced many musical instruments, including the harp, into China from western Asia at that time.

CHAPTER 1

TWO TEACHERS
BUDDHA, KONGZI, AND EARLY INDIA AND CHINA

In a city near the foothills of the Himalaya Mountains, in what is now the country of Nepal, around 535 BCE, a young prince slipped out of the royal palace in disguise. His name was Siddartha Gautama, and his parents had raised him in the palace so he would see only things that were rich and happy and beautiful. Overcome with curiosity about what lay beyond the palace walls, he put on ordinary clothes, walked out the gate, and strolled through the streets of the nearby city. He was deeply shocked to see, everywhere around him, signs of poverty, exploitation, illness, and old age. Life, he realized, was not at all what he had been led to believe. And because the ancient Indian religion of Brahminism taught that after death people were reborn into other lives and, so, lived many lifetimes, the suffering he had observed seemed endless.

Thinking about what he had seen, Siddartha came to the conclusion that while life may offer some temporary pleasures, it consists, in the end, of an endless cycle of birth, old age, sickness, and death. Siddartha sat down under an ancient tree considered to be holy by the local people and began to meditate, or think with deep concentration. After many days, he came upon what he saw as the ultimate truth: that life as we know it is an illusion, but people believe in the illusion because they want the world to be real. They are slaves to their own desires, and so they cannot escape from suffering. Moreover karma, the burden of all that one has ever done, follows every individual from lifetime to lifetime, making escape from suffering even more difficult.

Transformed by this experience, Siddartha became known as the Buddha (the Enlightened One), and set out to teach others about his insights. He called his basic idea the

Four Noble Truths: "All of life involves suffering; the source of suffering is desire; the way to stop suffering is to extinguish desire; the method for extinguishing desire is to follow the Noble Eightfold Path." These truths became a fundamental part of the Buddha's teaching, and people believe these are his own words, even though there is no copy of his actual writing. That path, he taught, consists of right views, right intentions, right speech, right action, right livelihood, right effort, right mindfulness, and right concentration. Right views and intentions add up to wisdom; right speech, action, and livelihood (that is, one's way of making a living) lead to good moral conduct; and right effort, mindfulness, and concentration produce spiritual development. This teaching became the Buddhist dharma, meaning "truth" and "duty." The result of following the dharma, for the believer, is to escape from the endless cycle of rebirth and suffering, and to become part of the great force of the universe itself.

During the rest of his lifetime, the Buddha converted many people to the new religion that we call Buddhism, and he set up many communities of believers so that they could encourage one another to follow the eightfold path to salvation.

MASTER KONG

A few years after Siddhartha left home, another remarkable individual was growing up in the small state of Lu in northeastern China. Kong Zhongni was born into a wealthy family with a long history of public service, and he received a good education as a child. Then he got a job with the government of Lu, but was frustrated when he was not promoted. He began to travel to other states, looking for a ruler who would give him a high position so he could try out a radical new approach to government that would bring peace to the land. He taught that government service should not be based on noble birth, but on intelligence, education, and virtue. "The noble-minded person loves virtue; the ordinary-minded person loves what serves his own interests." Zhongni could not find a ruler who was willing to try to put his ideas into practice.

A painting of scenes from the life of the Buddha shows the Buddha saying good-bye to his horse and servant as he prepares to leave behind his luxurious life as a prince (top). Below, two gods and five human companions visit the Buddha as he begins his new life as a wandering religious teacher. Missionaries used paintings to explain Buddhism to people who could not read the Buddhist scriptures for themselves.

Zhongni eventually returned to Lu, where he became a teacher. People began to call him Kongzi, or Master Kong. (In the West he is usually known as Confucius, a Latin name given to him by European Christian missionaries in China in the 17th century.) He hoped his students would eventually get government jobs and transform the way China was ruled. He emphasized the values of human kindness, justice, virtue, and respect for parents and ancestors. His ideal was a world in which all people belong to one big family, linked by bonds of trust, obligation, and obedience.

At the time when Kongzi lived, China was divided up into many competing smaller states. No single state was able to unify the country under its own rule. Many people had ideas about how to unite the country as it was supposed to have been in earlier times. Kongzi and his followers argued that good government was the key to bringing peace to the known world.

The Chinese were also interested in other ways of thought. One group of thinkers was the Daoists, followers of a semi-legendary figure named Laozi, which means Old Master. Daoists taught that everything in the universe follows the eternal Dao, or Way, a force that lies behind all process of change. They hoped for a ruler who would be so tuned in to the power of the Way that he could rule the world without even trying. The Legalists offered another opinion; they believed that if laws were clear and specific, everyone would do exactly what he or she was supposed to do. But for a long time, none of these ideas was enough to unify the known world.

At last the ruler of the powerful state of Qin, in northwestern China succeeded in uniting China by force in 221 BCE. He created a new title for himself: Qin Shi Huangdi, First Emperor of Qin. The First Emperor accomplished many things. He standardized the country's money and its written language. He

An imaginary portrait of Confucius, engraved on a stone tablet more than a thousand years after his death, shows him as an elderly official wearing a tall hat. For more than 2,000 years, Confucius has been admired in China as a great teacher whose ideas formed the foundation of Chinese government and society.

built a wall to protect the country's northern frontier. (This was an early version of the Great Wall that exists in China today.) Hoping to live well in the spirit world after his death, he built a huge tomb for himself, guarded by an army of thousands of clay soldiers. His tomb and its clay warriors, near the city of Xi'an in northwestern China, are now regarded as one of the wonders of the ancient world. He also encouraged good farming practices and built canals and systems for watering the crops. But his laws were so harsh that people soon rebelled against him. When he died in 210 BCE, his son was soon overthrown. After a period of warfare, a new dynasty, or ruling family, called the Han, united the country again. They ruled China for more than 400 years.

Shaped like a stylized knife, this ancient Chinese coin from around 350 BCE was made by pouring melted bronze into a clay mold. The Chinese used coins of several different shapes before the Qin dynasty created a standard currency: a round coin with a square hole in the center.

KINGS AND SAINTS

Meanwhile, in India, centuries after the Buddha's lifetime, his followers divided into two main branches. Some followed Theravada, the "Teaching of the Elders" (also called Hinayana or "Lesser Vehicle"). They believed that you must leave your family, become a monk, live frugally, and follow the example of the Buddha in order to attain enlightenment. Others created a new school, called Mahayana (the "Great Vehicle"). They said that you could become enlightened without leaving the world of your family and friends. Mahayana teachers developed the idea of the Bodhisattva, a kind of saint who postpones his own enlightenment in order to help others reach salvation. This made it possible for many ordinary people to believe in and practice Buddhism without altering their daily lives too much. Both Theravada and Mahayana Buddhism spread from India to other places, Theravada especially to Southeast Asia and Mahayana especially to Central Asia and from there to China, Korea, and Japan.

Another new religion, Jainism, was founded in northeastern India by Mahavira, who lived around the same time as Siddhartha Gautama. Like Siddhartha, Mahavira was a

Ancients and moderns have different customs; the present and the past follow different courses of action. To attempt to apply a benevolent and lenient government to the people in a desperate age is about the same as trying to drive wild horses without reins.

—Hanfeizi, Legalist philosopher, from The Book of Hanfeizi, about 240 BCE

The Promise of Buddhahood

66 | **VERSES FROM THE LOTUS SUTRA, ABOUT 100 BCE**

Buddhist holy texts are called sutras, which means "threads." There are hundreds of sutras, written at different times, in different places, and in several languages, but believers accept them all as the Buddha's real teaching. One of the most important sutras of the Mahayana school of Buddhism is the Lotus Sutra. The Central Asian monk Kumarajiva translated the Lotus Sutra into Chinese in the fifth century CE, and it became a key element in winning acceptance for Buddhism in China. These verses express the believer's joy in the prospect of Buddhahood.

When I hear the Buddha's gentle voice,
Profound, far removed from the ordinary understanding,
extremely subtle,
Setting forth the pure Dharma,
My heart is overjoyed.
My doubts and second thoughts are cleared away forever,
And I dwell securely in the midst of real knowledge, saying:
"Of a certainty I shall become a Buddha,
Revered by gods and men."

On this page from a 10th-century Chinese translation of the Lotus Sutra, a convicted criminal wears a heavy wooden collar as punishment. Kneeling next to the criminal, a man, perhaps the criminal's father, prays to Guanyin, the Bodhisattva of Infinite Mercy, for help in their time of trouble.

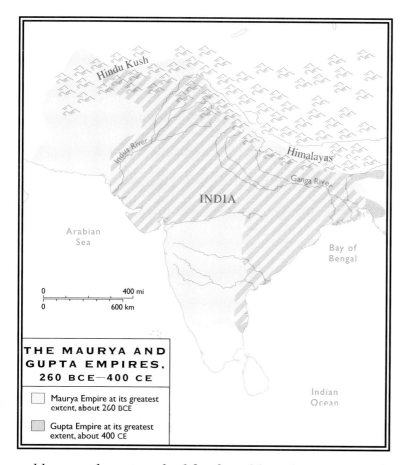

THE MAURYA AND
GUPTA EMPIRES,
260 BCE—400 CE

Maurya Empire at its greatest
extent, about 260 BCE

Gupta Empire at its greatest
extent, about 400 CE

nobleman who rejected a life of wealth and power to seek religious salvation. Mahavira taught that time repeats itself endlessly in cycles of millions of years. Mahavira and his followers encouraged believers to live in religious communities where they would strive for *moksha,* liberation from worldly existence after death. The most important practice of Jainism is *ahimsa,* "doing no harm" to other living creatures. Jains are all strict vegetarians and they take care not to harm even the smallest of insects.

At the same time that these new religions were being founded, big changes were taking place in the ancient Brahmin religion of India. These changes made Indian religion (later called Hinduism) more a matter of personal faith and practice and less a matter for religious specialists and priests. Hinduism has many gods, and the gods can appear in many forms; but there are three gods who tower above the rest. They are Brahma, the creator of the world; Vishnu, the sustainer of the world; and Shiva, the destroyer of the world. Three gods are needed, because, according to Hindu belief, the world is created, sustained, destroyed, and created again countless times, over and over for millions and millions of years. Hinduism teaches that every individual soul is a reflection of the great world-soul personified by the gods.

Hinduism, like Buddhism, emphasizes the concept of dharma: "truth" and "duty." Every person has a dharma that he or she can express by devotion to a god and by living a virtuous life. An individual's dharma, in turn, is expressed in the context of that person's community and social position. Hindu society is based on the idea of caste, the idea that everyone is born into their position in life. The four main castes are priests, warriors, merchants, and farmers. (Importantly, both Buddhism and Jainism reject the idea of caste, so that in those religions, all believers are equal.)

The peoples of India speak many different languages and have many different cultural traditions, and have often

A stone pillar in northern India is topped by a statue of a lion. King Ashoka, who ruled the Maurya dynasty from about 272 to 232 BCE, set up numerous pillars of this kind, engraved with his laws and proclamations so that they could be visible to everyone in the kingdom.

lived under many different states. Sometimes, however, a strong leader would create a large state, or an empire, that united much of the Indian subcontinent. Around 324 BCE, for example, Chandragupta Maurya united much of the Indian subcontinent in the Maurya Empire, which at its height included most of India and parts of present-day Afghanistan, Pakistan, and Bangladesh. The Maurya Empire's greatest ruler, King Ashoka, who ruled from around 272 to 232 BCE, is remembered as a strong supporter of Buddhism. He provided funds to build thousands of temples and stupas (buildings to hold holy objects), and promoted the spread of Buddhism throughout India and into Central Asia and Southeast Asia. Referring to himself, he said in an edict carved on a stone tablet, "The Beloved of the Gods desires safety, self-control, justice and happiness for all beings."

Religion and military power were not enough to keep the Maurya Empire together, and early in the second century BCE India split into many states again. From about 320 to 500 CE, much of northern India was united again in the Gupta Empire. But whether under one empire or many kingdoms, India's influence in the world grew. Indian merchants traveled to the northwest through the Indus River Valley and across the Khyber Pass to trade with kingdoms in Central Asia. Merchants who lived in coastal cities traveled by ship to the lands near the Persian Gulf and the Red Sea, bringing cotton cloth, spices, and other goods to the Middle East and as far as Rome. Other merchants went by ship to trade with kingdoms throughout Southeast Asia, bringing Hinduism and Buddhism into that region along with Indian cloth and other goods.

GOT SILK?

The rulers of China's Han dynasty, which was in power from 206 BCE to 220 CE, gave priority to two projects that had an enormous influence on China's future: Confucian government and trade on the Silk Road. The most powerful of the Han rulers, Emperor Wu, who ruled from 140 to 87 BCE, created a stable, centralized system of government that made it possible to unify and control a large empire for long periods of time. He took his ideas about government from several schools of thought. His law and management techniques came from the Legalists; his reliance on spiritual power came from the Daoists; and, most important, his belief that education and virtue should be the basis of government came from Kongzi. This new, combined political philosophy is what scholars today call "Confucianism," though it

Benevolence is difficult; he who performs a benevolent act accomplishes something difficult. I have performed much that is benevolent. Benevolence shall also be practiced by my sons, my grandsons and their descendants, even until the very dissolution of the universe.

—King Ashoka, Indian ruler, inscription on a stone tablet, about 240 BCE

Mengzi visited King Hui of Liang. The king said, "Sir, you have not minded coming a thousand miles to visit me. I assume you have something that will be of profit to my kingdom." Mengzi replied, "Why must Your Majesty speak of profit? I bring humaneness and righteousness, that's all."

—Mengzi, Confucian philosopher, *The Book of Mengzi*, about 320 BCE

included ideas that went beyond the original teachings of Kongzi. The most far-reaching effect of Confucianism in the Han period was the use of examinations to select public officials on the basis of their knowledge and virtue.

Emperor Wu started the Silk Road trade to deal with a military problem. Horse-riding nomadic warriors threatened the Han's northern frontier, and often raided areas within the long walls inherited from the Qin and reconstructed by the Han. The Han defended its territory with foot soldiers armed with spears, swords, and crossbows. Emperor Wu realized that in order to fight the nomads more effectively, China also needed cavalry, or horse troops. He sent an official named Zhang Qian to explore the lands to the west of China where there were many horses. Zhang Qian was away for 12 years and traveled thousands of miles on foot and on horseback.

When he returned home, Zhang Qian told the emperor that the people of Central Asia wanted as much Chinese silk as they could get, and had a large supply of excellent war horses available for sale. China had plenty of silk. The emperor sent officials with camel-loads of silk to Central Asia to trade for horses. This was a big success, and from about 100 BCE on, trade along what came to be called the Silk Road grew rapidly.

Soon Chinese silk was being sold in the markets of the Middle East and even Rome, while Roman, Greek, Persian, Indian and other foreign goods and ideas reached China.

After trade started between China and western Asia, Buddhism soon spread to the cities of Central Asia along the Silk Road, and from there eastward to China. Buddhism reached Luoyang, the capital city of Han overland from Central Asia in the

Excavated from a tomb in northwestern China, this bronze statuette of a man on horseback dates to the end of the Han dynasty, around 220. The Chinese government started trade on the Silk Road during the Han dynasty to buy sturdy war horses for its armed forces.

mid-first century CE. At first Buddhism was not well under-stood in China, but eventually it began to catch on. Meanwhile, Daoism, influenced by Buddhism, also developed into an organized religion, with temples, priests, rituals, and sacred texts.

After more than 400 years in power, the Han dynasty finally collapsed in 220 CE. Torn apart by warfare, China was again divided into competing kingdoms. No one was able to unify China again for more than 350 years. For most of that time peoples from the northern grasslands who conquered territories south of the Great Wall ruled northern China. Many Chinese intellectuals, disillusioned with a government run by powerful families and corrupt officials became Buddhist monks instead of trying to become government officials. Buddhism became more and more popular in China, and soon spread from China to Korea and Japan.

A family portrait, with women on the left and men on the right, was painted in a Buddhist cave-shrine at Dunhuang, in northwestern China, in 983. The family, rather than the individual person, was the basic unit of Chinese society, and Confucians considered society as a whole to be one big family.

India at the end of the Gupta period and China after the fall of the Han dynasty were both politically divided but culturally strong. India's influence extended into Central Asia by land, and to the Middle East and Southeast Asia by sea. China's influence extended along the Silk Road into Central Asia, as well as northeastward to Korea and Japan. From its origins in India, Buddhism spread throughout Asia to become one of the great world religions.

Carved from stone on a hillside in southwestern China, a huge statue of Buddha lies on its side, accompanied by smaller statues of Bodhisattvas, or Mahayana Buddhist saints. For several centuries after it arrived in China from India, Buddhism was strongly influenced by Chinese ideas, such as Confucianism and Daoism, and by Chinese styles of art.

CHAPTER 2

CHINA UNITED, AGAIN
THE SUI AND TANG DYNASTIES

China in the late sixth century CE was a dangerous place to be a ruler or a high official. The life expectancy of dynasties was short, betrayal and rebellion were common, and losers in the game of politics were likely to wind up dead. On the other hand, many ambitious men dreamed of reuniting China for the first time since the fall of the Han dynasty in 220 CE. They knew that the man who accomplished this would become Son of Heaven, the ruler of the known world. In 589 CE, one man, Yang Jian, succeeded—

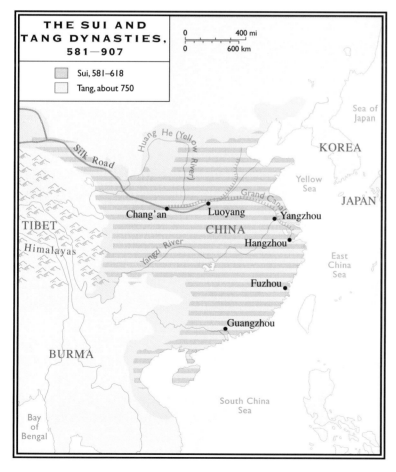

through boldness, intelligence, and good luck—in realizing that ambition.

Yang Jian was born in 541. His father was the Duke of Sui, the head of an old, wealthy, and powerful Buddhist family of mixed Chinese and Turkish ancestry. In his teens, Yang Jian was appointed to various posts in the government of the Northern Zhou dynasty, which then ruled most of northern China. When Yang's father died, the young man became the new Duke of Sui, and he was made a general in the Northern Zhou army. The Northern Zhou emperor died in 578, and soon afterward Yang Jian seized power by naming himself regent, or substitute ruler, for the infant prince who was the next rightful emperor. Yang spent the next two years in battles to eliminate the rest of the Northern Zhou princes. In 580 he made himself prime minister of the Northern Zhou government, and in 581 he arranged for the boy emperor to give up the throne, bringing the Northern Zhou to an end.

In the same year, Yang Jian proclaimed himself the first emperor of the new Sui dynasty, with authority over "all under heaven." He put on the imperial robes, held his first court audience, and executed 59 members of the former Northern Zhou royal family. At first he ruled only the northern part of China, but in 589 he defeated the Chen dynasty, which had controlled the south. He thus succeeded in uniting all of China, ending a period of disunion that had lasted more than 350 years.

SUI SUCCEEDS, AT FIRST

Despite his bloody rise to power, Yang Jian became known as Sui Wendi, "civil emperor of Sui." Perhaps this was because he followed the example of the Han ruler named Wendi and anchored his policies in a kind of Confucianism that also included elements of Daoist and Legalist thinking. Sui Wendi selected government officials on the basis of their ability, and used them, more than recent dynasties had, to weaken the influence of powerful noble families. The new ruler also strongly supported Buddhism, and used it to support his claim to be a universal ruler. In 585 he issued a public proclamation that "Buddha entrusts the universal law to princes of states. . . . We accept Buddha's trust."

In retrospect, the Sui dynasty seems very much like the Qin dynasty, which ruled China 800 years earlier. Both unified China after long periods of disunion, but neither dynasty was able to hold onto power for very long. Like the First Emperor of Qin, Sui Wendi and his son Yangdi (who inherited the throne in 604) tried to do too much, too quickly. They built the Grand Canal, a 700-mile-long waterway that extended from the capital city of Chang'an, west of the great bend of the Huang He (Yellow River) in northern China, all the way to the mouth of the Yangzi River near present-day Shanghai, on the east-central coast. It was designed to bring grain from the rich rice-producing regions of the south to the north. It also allowed Yangdi to make frequent visits in his imperial barge to the warm, green southern lands, which he much preferred to the dry and dusty north.

The Sui rulers also tried to extend the Chinese empire by conquering Korea. These ambitious projects placed a heavy burden on the common people. They were used to being asked to spend several weeks a year doing unpaid work on public projects, and they understood that men had to serve for several years in the army. But the canal required tens of thousands of laborers to work for months on end, and soldiers spent years in the army fighting the bloody and unsuccessful Korean campaign. The common people had no time left to do their own work, farming, so they came to resent the Sui rulers.

When a huge flood of the Huang He in 618 led to a deadly famine, people openly said that the Sui dynasty was a failure; perhaps the Sui rulers did not have the Mandate of Heaven—the natural right to rule—after all. As a classic Confucian book, the *Venerated Documents*, says, "Heaven hears and sees as the people hear and see." Soon peasant rebellions broke out in

Sui Wendi, who was of mixed Turkish and Han background, reunified China in 589, after more than three centuries of division. Wendi and his son overburdened the people with military expeditions to Korea and unpaid labor on the Grand Canal, and the dynasty was overthrown by popular uprisings.

Yangdi, the second ruler of the Sui dynasty, completed construction of the Grand Canal and enjoyed sailing to and from his secondary capital at Yangzhou. Later historians blamed the fall of the dynasty on such expensive practices, and Yangdi became a model of the "bad last emperor," responsible for losing his dynasty's mandate of heaven.

the central plain. The leader of one of those rebellions came from a very high position within the Sui government.

THE TANG TAKES UP THE TASK

Li Yuan was the head of an old and powerful Turkish-Chinese family, related by marriage to the Sui imperial family. He controlled a strong army in a principality in northern China called Tang, and Sui Yangdi began to suspect him of disloyalty. Facing arrest on charges of conspiracy anyway, Li Yuan and his son Li Shimin decided to rebel. They quickly made alliances with other rebel armies, captured the Sui capital, and proclaimed their own Tang dynasty in 618.

Li Yuan proved to be a very capable ruler, but his son Li Shimin was in a hurry to become emperor himself. In 626 he had his elder brother (who was next in line for the throne) murdered, forced his father to retire, and took the throne as the second Tang emperor. Usually known by his imperial title, Tang Taizong (Great Ancestor), he ruled for 22 years. Despite the bloody beginning of his reign, he is usually considered to have been one of the best emperors in all Chinese history.

Tang Taizong surrounded himself with intelligent and outspoken advisers. Although aristocrats held many positions at the highest level of government, the emperor also extended and improved the old idea of selecting officials (men only) through examinations; written exams were held regularly all over the realm. Those who passed were granted degrees (like diplomas or college degrees) that made them eligible for government jobs. One result was that many boys received good educations to prepare for the exams. At the age of five or six they started to learn the Confucian classics—ancient works of philosophy, history, and literature from which Confucian thinkers drew their basic ideas. Even those who did not pass the exams became part of a growing class of highly educated men, which was good for the country in general. Confucian education also encouraged participation in the arts, such as literature, painting, and calligraphy, the practice of beautiful writing.

Another Tang policy was land reform designed to give every farmer an approximately equal amount of land. Although not completely successful, because it was too complicated to manage, the equal field system, as it was called, improved the lives of ordinary people and increased agricultural production. For example, land reform stimulated investors to put money and labor toward creating additional rice fields in the Yangzi River valley, and the increased harvest of rice could be brought to northern China by boat on the Grand Canal. City workers also benefited from Tang policies, as increased trade created more jobs for merchants and craft workers.

Tang Taizong also supported Buddhism. By the early Tang period, Buddhism had been in China for almost six centuries, and had become thoroughly Chinese. New types of Buddhism had arisen in China, such as the Pure Land school, which encouraged devotion to the Bodhisattva (Buddhist

Li Shimin, an ambitious son of the Tang founder, killed his elder brother to become emperor in the early seventh century. But Li Shimin governed so wisely, that later generations of statesmen and officials in China, Korea, Vietnam, and Japan regarded him as a model ruler.

We monks, having in mind merely our longing for the Buddhist teachings, have come from afar to this benevolent land with our hearts set on sacred places and our spirits rejoicing in the pilgrimage.

—Ennin, Japanese Buddhist monk visiting China, in his diary, 840

saint) of Infinite Mercy. But people were also confused about various teachings of different branches of Buddhism, which sometimes seemed to contradict each other. A young Chinese monk named Xuanzang traveled to India in 629 to study and bring copies of important sutras (Buddhist scriptures) back to China. When Xuanzang returned in 645, the emperor welcomed him personally and ordered his officials to build a special pagoda, a multistoried tower at a Buddhist temple, in the capital city of Chang'an to hold the new sutras. Xuanzang was a real person, but stories of his travels have become fantastic legends in which he is threatened by sorcerers or captured by monsters. Those legends have made Xuanzang a beloved figure in Chinese popular literature.

Buddhism also encouraged one of the most important discoveries in world history: the invention of printing. Chinese people wanted copies of the Buddhist scriptures, but each book had to be copied by hand, which was slow and difficult. Early in the Tang period, some unknown Buddhist craftsperson hit upon the idea of carving words and pictures (in mirror image) onto smooth blocks of wood. The wood blocks could then be coated with ink, and the images transferred to a sheet of paper (which the Chinese had also invented, centuries earlier, during the Han dynasty). Thus multiple copies of any written material could be printed quickly and cheaply. Like many good ideas, the invention caught on quickly and was soon in widespread use.

Buddhism also popularized tea drinking in China. Tea had been known there for centuries, but before the Tang dynasty it was not a common drink. During the Tang dynasty, Buddhist monks adopted the custom of drinking tea to stay alert during long religious ceremonies. They also served it to guests instead of alcoholic beverages, which monks were not supposed to drink. As a monk named Guanxu wrote in a poem,

> In a deep brazier I heat an iron flask,
> The tea, blended with bitter herbs, is warming.
> The fire, fed with cedar roots, is fragrant. . . .
> A good heap of sutras is read through.

The custom of drinking tea soon spread throughout society, and China became a land of tea drinkers.

The early Tang emperors expanded the size of their empire as much as they could. They built a series of military bases westward along the Silk Road, eventually as far as the Pamir Mountains in what is now Afghanistan. Like the Sui emperors, Tang Taizong also tried and failed to conquer Korea. Korea remained independent, but China influenced

The Buddha speaks with his students on this page from the Diamond Sutra, which was printed in 868, making it the world's oldest complete printed book. The Chinese invented wood-block printing to spread the Buddhist faith, and it became the most efficient means of reproducing Chinese texts for the next thousand years.

Korean culture and Korea helped to transmit Chinese goods and ideas to its eastern neighbor, Japan.

Trade along the Silk Road enriched China in many ways. The Chinese sent silk, herbal medicines, ceramics, and other local products westward by caravan, and received exotic things in return. From Persia (modern-day Iran) and the Middle East, they received new kinds of musical instruments, and musicians to play them, as well as gold and silver cups, bowls, and vases. From India they imported cotton cloth. From Byzantium (the eastern capital of the Roman Empire, today the city of Istanbul in Turkey) came glassware and jewelry. Chinese merchants also traded some of these imported goods eastward to Korea and Japan.

A CROWING HEN

Probably the most remarkable of all the Tang rulers was a woman named Wu Zhao, who became the only female emperor in Chinese history. In 640, as a young woman, she was presented by her parents to the imperial palace to serve as one of the emperor's many concubines, or junior wives. Bright, well educated, and ambitious, as well as attractive, she quickly became one of Emperor Taizong's favorite wives. When he died, she became a favorite of his son, the

Wu Zhao was the only woman in Chinese history to hold the position of emperor. She used a Buddhist text to justify her authority and commissioned artists to carve many stone images of the Buddha. This one was said to resemble her.

Now Buddha was a man of the barbarians who did not speak the language of China and wore clothes of a different fashion. His sayings did not concern the ways of our ancient kings.

—Tang Confucian intellectual Han Yü, "Memorial on the Bone of the Buddha," about 820

new emperor, and had children with him. She arranged to have the emperor's number one wife, the first or most important wife, murdered.

Wu Zhao became the number one wife, and when her husband was crippled by a stroke, she ran the government for him for the rest of his life. As a later history, *The Comprehensive Mirror for Aid in Government*, put it, "The great powers of all under heaven devolved on the empress. Promotion and demotion, life or death, were settled by her word. The emperor sat with folded hands [unable to do anything]." When the emperor died in 683, she continued to rule as regent for one of her sons. Then, in 690, Wu Zhao proclaimed herself emperor, and even changed the name of the dynasty. Reviving the name of an ancient dynasty that had ruled China more than a thousand years earlier, she called herself the "Holy and Divine Emperor of the Zhou Dynasty."

In China there was an old saying that a female ruler was like a hen crowing—something that was unnatural, if not impossible. But Empress Wu was a capable ruler who governed China effectively for 15 years. She retired from the throne and died at the age of 80, in 705 CE. Power returned to the Tang imperial family.

Tang Xuanzong, who ruled from 713 to 756, was capable and deeply supportive of the arts. The early years of his long reign are remembered as a time of exceptional brilliance in Chinese culture. But he also made a serious error of judgment that almost destroyed the Tang dynasty. The emperor fell madly in love with his favorite concubine, Yang Guifei. He began spending all his time with her, paying no attention

*Yesterday's man on top of
the wall
Beneath the wall is a ghost
today.
Still the banners are like an
array of stars;
And the war drums' sound is
not yet done;
And out of my family, husbands and sons,
All are there in the sound of
the drums.*

—Tang poet Li Bai, "Fighting
South of the Wall, No. 2,"
about 755

to his official duties; worse, he gave high official positions to some of her relatives, who soon proved to be lazy and corrupt. Leading members of the government were outraged, but the emperor wouldn't listen to them. With the central government in turmoil, the emperor's most powerful general, An Lushan, rebelled in 755, plunging the country into civil war. The emperor had to flee from the capital and give up the throne. He lived for several years in exile in the southwestern province of Sichuan. The Tang, assisted by foreign troops, defeated the rebellion in 763, and the Tang dynasty survived, but it never completely recovered its earlier glory.

Despite these political troubles, the Tang dynasty was the greatest era in Chinese history for poetry, and the best poets of the Tang period lived during the eighth century. In the first half of the century Wang Wei, who turned his back on luxury to live a simple Buddhist life, wrote serious, religious poetry. His friend Li Bai also wrote Buddhist verse, but is best known for his poems celebrating food and drink, travel, friendship, and other pleasures in life. Du Fu, who was just a bit younger than Li Bai, lived through the disastrous An Lushan rebellion, and many of his poems reflect the sorrow of the times. In one poem he thinks of his wife and family, from whom he has been separated by the fighting:

In Fuzhou, far away, my wife is watching
The moon alone tonight, and my thoughts fill
With sadness for my children, who can't think
Of me here in Chang'an; they're too young still.
Her cloud-soft hair is moist with fragrant mist.
In the clear light her white arms sense the chill.
When will we feel the moonlight dry our tears,
Leaning together on our window-sill?

During the final century of Tang rule, the Chinese began to lose control of the Silk Road in Central Asia, and foreign goods and ideas became less common in everyday life. Some intellectuals began criticizing Buddhism as a "barbarian" (meaning foreign and uncultured) religion—even though it had been part of Chinese life for centuries. These thinkers interpreted the Confucian classics in new ways to

Death of an Imperial Favorite

" BAI JUYI, "SONG OF UNENDING SORROW," ABOUT 820

Bai Juyi, one of the most accomplished poets of the late Tang dynasty, wrote a long poem called "Song of Unending Sorrow" about the ill-fated love affair between Tang Xuanzong and his beautiful concubine Yang Guifei. This section describes how, when rebellion broke out and the emperor, the Son of Heaven, fled into exile, his imperial guards refused to go with him until he agreed to allow them to execute Yang Guifei.

> From the ninefold palace wall rose plumes of dust and smoke.
> A thousand wagons, ten thousand horsemen, travelled
>   southwestwards
> With the royal banners waving. But then they halted,
> West of the capital, not more than a hundred miles.
> The six-division army would go no further, no matter the danger,
> Until he gave up his moth-browed beauty to die, trampled by
>   horses.
> Her gold-flowered hair combs fell to the ground, her kingfisher-
>   feather crown,
> Her trembling bird-ornaments of gold, her jade hairpins;
> The Son of Heaven could only cover his eyes, unable to help her,
> As blood and tears flowed together.
> Dust swirled in yellow clouds, the wind blew cold,
> As the exile-road wound upwards over Sword Watchtower Pass.

The Tang emperor Xuanzong supported many artists at his court, and probably commissioned this painting. In it, he watches the woman he loves, Yang Guifei, mount her horse. Many Tang women rode horseback, but few were of such high status as to be assisted by one official, one groom, two maids, and two other attendants standing nearby.

find answers to big questions about the meaning of life and how to organize a good society. This renewed form of Confucianism would become very important in the period after the end of the Tang dynasty.

Beginning in the 830s, the Tang dynasty began experiencing the problems typical of a regime that has lasted too long. Corruption, tax evasion, and rising land rents created injustices that fell most heavily on the common people. Scattered rebellions broke out, and from 875 to 884 the rebel leader Huang Chao led a full-scale uprising. This rebellion resulted in the death of millions of people and virtually destroyed the old Tang noble class. The last Tang emperors struggled on until 907, when the final one was overthrown by another rebellion. Half a century would pass before another successful dynasty was established.

A bodhisattva, a Buddhist who has attained enlightenment but stays in the world to help save others, is here depicted as much larger than life size to indicate her spiritual power. She is leading an aristocratic woman of the late Tang, with powdered face, reddened lips, and shaped eyebrows, toward the Pure Land (paradise), visible in the top left corner of the painting.

CHAPTER 3

RAJAS AND SULTANS
THE STRUGGLE FOR INDIA

In the small kingdom of Shivamogga, in southwestern India, sometime about 1140 CE, a young girl named Mahadeviyakka decided to devote her life to the Hindu god Shiva. Leaving home against her parents' will, she became a wanderer. Paying no attention to such things as food and clothing, she composed poetry and songs in praise of Shiva, whom she always called "the Lord white as jasmine" (jasmine is a white, sweet-smelling flower). The king of Shivamogga saw how beautiful she was and insisted on marrying her, but Mahadeviyakka would have nothing to do with him. She expressed her feelings in a poem:

> So the immortal Lord white as jasmine is my husband:
> Take these husbands who die,
> Decay, and feed them to the kitchen fires.

For years she lived sometimes alone and sometimes in religious communities. Then one day she walked off into the hills and disappeared. She was not yet 30 years old. She is still remembered and loved by millions of Hindus for the inspirational beauty of her poetry:

> A vein of sapphires
> hides in the earth,
> a sweetness in fruit.
>
> and in plain-looking rock
> lies a golden ore,
> and in seeds,
> the treasure of oil.
>
> Like these,
> the Infinite
> rests concealed in the heart.
>
> No one can see the ways
> of our jasmine-white Lord.

Mahadeviyakka's religious commitment was a response to the very complicated world of India in her time, when the whole subcontinent was deeply divided by geography, by language and ethnicity, and by religion.

The geography of South Asia—including today's India, Pakistan, Nepal, and Bangladesh—is very diverse, and supports many different ways of life. The lowlands of the Ganga and Brahmaputra River valleys in the northeast are excellent for growing rice. Rice is also grown in coastal areas in the southeast and the southwest. In the drier plains of the north-central region, and in the Indus River valley of the northwest, people raise wheat and cattle; in the south-central highlands people grow other kinds of grain, such as millet. Some parts of the northwest are grasslands or semi-desert, where pastoral nomads raise camels, sheep,

Narasimha-varman II, a king of Pallava who ruled from 680 to 720, used the wealth he earned from overseas trade to fund the building of numerous ornate temples to Shiva. This temple, carved from solid rock, is located at Mamallapuram, the seaport in eastern India that was an important jumping off point to Southeast Asia.

and goats. Parts of the southwestern coast, in contrast, are wetlands where the main crop is coconut. All along the coast people have fished since ancient times, and also traveled by boat to trade overseas.

The geographic and economic diversity of India is matched by diversity in language and cultures. People of hundreds of different ethnic groups speak different languages, wear different styles of clothing, and enjoy different foods. Some people are Hindus, some Jains, and some Buddhists, though Buddhism faded in importance in India after about the ninth century CE. By the early eighth century, some Indians began to adopt a completely new religion—Islam—that had arrived from the Middle East. All this made it very difficult to unify India. The fact that it was difficult did not keep some people from trying.

This statue of a seated founder of the Jain religion, sculpted from white marble in northwestern India in the 11th century, quietly celebrates the principle of non-violence, or doing no harm, that is central to that faith. The religion appealed to kings and merchants through Indian history; in the 20th century, it inspired the Indian leader Mahatma Gandhi.

KING HARSHA

One who tried was Harsha Vardhana. Harsha was born in 590, the son of a local king whose kingdom was located on the dry north-central plain. The kingdom's capital was near the Jamuna River, a large and important river that flows eastward and joins the Ganga River (the Ganges), the waters of which are considered sacred by Hindus and Buddhists alike. Harsha's father had grand political ambitions, partly because he was descended on his mother's side from the Gupta dynasty, which had ruled northern India in centuries past. But his son's ambitions were even grander. Not contented with being just a raja (king) like his father, Harsha gave himself a title that meant "great king of kings."

When Harsha's father died, the young prince was forced to engage in a series of wars to keep others from taking over his family's state. His brother, the crown prince, was killed in battle, so Harsha became the new king. Another king

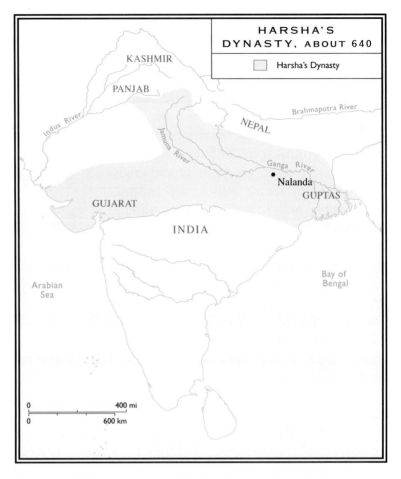

HARSHA'S
DYNASTY, ABOUT 640

Harsha's Dynasty

KASHMIR

PANJAB

Indus River

Jamuna River

Brahmaputra River

NEPAL

Ganga River

Nalanda

GUPTAS

GUJARAT

INDIA

Arabian
Sea

Bay of
Bengal

0   400 mi
0   600 km

kidnapped his sister, and his brother-in-law died trying to rescue her. Harsha then led an army to rescue his sister himself. We know something about what happened next because of the Chinese monk Xuanzang, whose studies in Harsha's Buddhist kingdom were disrupted by these wars. According to Xuanzang's book about his travels, Harsha "went from east to west, subduing all who were not obedient. The elephants were never unharnessed, nor did the soldiers ever unbuckle their armor [because they were constantly at war]." After many years of fighting, Harsha controlled most of northern India. But his achievement lasted only a short time. The empire he built quickly fell apart after his death in 647.

Other kingdoms rose and fell in northern India after King Harsha's time. Beginning in the early eighth century, rulers from the Middle East challenged the kingdoms of India. These conquerors brought the religion of Islam to southern Asia for the first time.

ISLAM AND INDIA

Around 610 CE, in the city of Mecca in Arabia, a merchant named Muhammad believed that God had selected him to transmit God's final teachings to the world. Mecca was an important trading center whose population included both Jews and Christians, and Muhammad was much influenced by their beliefs. He regarded his God (whom he called Allah—a word that simply means "God") as the same God who appeared to Abraham in the Hebrew Bible. Muhammad's new teachings came to be called Islam, which means "submission" (to the will of God). A Muslim is "one who submits." Like many Christians and Buddhists, many Muslims feel a strong obligation to tell others about their message of salvation. Devoted Muslims spread their religion quickly, and within a century of Muhammad's death in 632 the Islamic world included most of the Middle East and North Africa.

Because for hundreds of years there had been trade and other contact between the Middle East and India, both overland and by sea, India was a natural place for Islam to spread. In 712, the Arab prince Muhammad ibn Qasim led an army across the Indus River to conquer the important cities of Sind (a kingdom in what is now Pakistan). Muhammad ibn Qasim then had to decide how to treat the local people. In their conquests, the Muslims gave favorable treatment to Jews and Christians, who were called People of the Book (that is, believers in the Bible). Muslims might extend this special treatment to others who believed in a single god, such as members of the ancient Zoroastrian religion of Persia. Most Muslims were much less tolerant of religions such as Hinduism and Buddhism, which allowed for many gods. According to a Persian historian, however, ibn Qasim respected Buddhist and Hindu temples "as if they were the churches of the Christians, the synagogues of

In the cool woods, where the bees seek flowers, Women, bright-bangled and garlanded, drink The sap of the palm and the pale sugar-cane, And the juice of the coconut which grows in the sand, Then running they plunge into the sea.

—Anonymous, "A Village Festival," poem from *Eight Anthologies,* a collection of poems in the Tamil language of southeastern India, sixth century

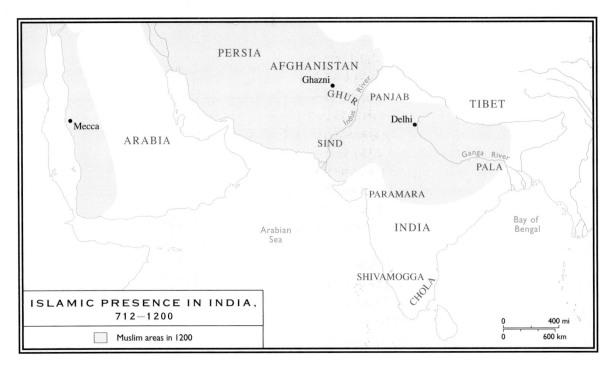

ISLAMIC PRESENCE IN INDIA,
712–1200

Muslim areas in 1200

the Jews, or the fire temples of the Zoroastrians." He thereby wisely avoided angering the local people.

The Arab conquest of Sind did not immediately affect the rest of India, but it changed the Islamic world, which now had direct access to Indian math and science. Two concepts that had an immediate impact were a simplified way of writing numbers (what we call Arabic numerals, but which are really Indian numerals) and the concept of zero as a number. Zero is one of the most basic and far-reaching ideas in mathematics. It is easy to see why mathematics, in Arabic, is called *hindisat,* "the Indian art."

For 500 years, from the early 8th to the early 13th century, the history of the Hindu kingdoms of northern India was a confusing and discouraging cycle of wars, conquests, and uprisings, with one royal family after another having a brief moment of glory before it too was overthrown. At the same time, northern India came under increasing threat of invasion from neighboring Islamic rulers, both in Sind and in what is now Afghanistan (where Islam largely replaced Buddhism in the 10th century).

SOUTH AND NORTH

Islam's impact on India was strongest in the northwest. In the northeast, too, Buddhism had been in decline for centuries. Nalanda University, founded in the fourth century, under the Gupta dynasty, had once trained thousands of students in Buddhist religion, literature, and art. By the end of the seventh century, Nalanda was in a state of decline and seemed to have lost much of its relevance. In the eighth century, however, a new state called Pala gave wholehearted support to Buddhism. With support from the Pala kings, Nalanda University flourished once again, and attracted students from all over Asia.

The Pala dynasty's power did not last long, and Buddhism in India continued its long-term decline. But the revival of Nalanda had one important effect: Monks from the university traveled to Tibet to introduce Buddhism to that high and remote kingdom beyond the Himalayas. There it developed a new branch called Tantra, which uses special symbols and rituals to visualize the struggle between

The priests, of whom there are several thousand, are men of the highest learning and talent. . . . From morning till night they engage in discussion; the old and the young mutually help one another.

—Chinese monk Xuanzang, visiting Nalanda University, *Journey to the West,* about 655.

This stupa, a windowless temple thought to contain the sacred remains of the Buddha, is part of the ruins of the Buddhist University at Nalanda, in northeast India. The university had a rebirth under the Pala dynasty and educated many learned monks who spread the faith throughout much of the rest of Asia.

The War God Battles a Demon

 KALIDASA, "THE BIRTH OF THE WAR GOD," ABOUT 400 CE

Kalidasa, who lived around 400 CE, worked at the court of the Gupta Empire and wrote in Sanskrit, the ancient classical language of northern India used by scholars and religious writers. His position in Indian literature is comparable to that of Shakespeare in English literature. Though he came from an ordinary family, his talent won him the attention of the royal court, and he became a prolific author of plays, stories, and poetry. Future generations memorized and recited his works. In this poem, "The Birth of the War God," Kalidasa describes a battle between Kumar, the god of war, and a terrible monster named Taraka. In these verses—a small portion of a very long poem—Taraka's army marches to attack Kumar but encounters a series of frightening visions and omens of defeat. This imaginary battle captures how the constant warfare between the kingdoms of ancient India must have felt in real life.

A fearful flock of evil birds,
Ready for the joy of eating the army of
    demons [Taraka's army]
Flew over the host of the gods,
And clouded the sun.

A wind continually fluttered their
    umbrellas and banners,
And troubled their eyes with clouds of
    whirling dust,
So that the trembling horses and ele-
    phants
And the great chariots could not be seen.

Suddenly monstrous serpents, as black as
    powdered soot,
Scattering poison from their upraised
    heads,
Frightful in form,
Appeared in the army's path.

The sun put on a ghastly robe
Of great and terrible snakes, curling
    together,
As if to mark his joy
At the death of the terrible demon.

And before the very disc of the sun
Jackals bayed harshly together,
As though eager fiercely to lap the blood
Of the king of the foes of the gods, fallen
    in battle. . . .

The host of the foe was jostled together.
The great elephants stumbled, the horses
    fell,
And all the foot soldiers clung together
    in fear,
As the earth trembled and the ocean rose
    to shake the mountains.

good and evil. In chanting ceremonies, for example, Tantric monks hold symbols such as lightning bolts made of bronze and ropes made of silk, to indicate their power to strike at evil with lightning and to tie up temptation to make it harmless.

In southern India, the most important state was the kingdom of Chola, which was founded around the third century CE and lasted for about a thousand years. It varied in size; sometimes it gained land when its armies conquered other states or its princes married princesses from neighboring states; sometimes it lost land when rival kingdoms conquered some of its territory. In general it controlled the southeastern coast and coastal plain, as well as the southern interior highlands. It grew rich from agriculture and from trade with Southeast Asia. Chola was known throughout India for the number and beauty of its Hindu temples, and for the exceptional quality of the stone and bronze sculptures that filled those temples.

A favorite theme of Chola sculpture was Shiva Natarajah (Lord of the Dance), which depicted the god Shiva dancing surrounded by a halo of flames. Many Hindus, such as the mystical poet Mahadeviyakka, devoted themselves to personal worship of Shiva. They believed that the world had been created through the energy of his dancing, and would continue to exist as long as he danced. When he stopped dancing the universe would vanish, paving the way for a new one to be created in its place. Temples such as the great Shiva temples of Chola were important centers of community life for the common people. On holidays they would be crowded with worshippers who came from miles around, dressed in their finest clothes, to participate in processions, prayers, and other ceremonies.

The mandala, a circular symbol representing the universe, was a powerful symbol in Tantric Buddhism, the form that became dominant in Tibet. Here a mandala appears on one wall of a 15th-century monastery in western Tibet, along with a chessboard-like painting on another wall, which contains a poem that can be read forwards or backwards, another sign of the order in the universe.

All subjects are dependent on their lord.
Only well-rooted trees bear fruit,
and only when the king is strong
do mens works prosper.

—Narayana, Indian poet, from the *Hitopadesa*, or "Salutary Instructions," a collection of poems and fables, 12th century

Chola and other states in southern India knew about the Islamic world but, to them, it seemed far away. In the north, however, the threat of Islamic conquest grew steadily more severe. During the 10th century, Islamic Turks established a kingdom at Gazni, in what is now Afghanistan. In 1004 their ruler, Mahmud of Gazni, led an army to seize Panjab (formerly spelled Punjab), the region of the upper reaches of the Indus River in northwestern India. His supporters saw this as an opportunity not merely to seize some of the wealth of India, but also to extend the reach of their Islamic faith. A Muslim scribe in his accounts of Mahmud's conquests praised God "for the honour [he] bestows upon Islam."

The Hindus, on the other hand, saw him as a fearsome conqueror. The same Muslim scribe quoted an Indian general who said that Mahmud "never contents himself with one blow of the sword." After one of his several invasions into the northern Indian heartland, Mahmud returned home with 350 elephants, 53,000 slaves, and vast amounts of gold, gemstones, and other wealth. He killed tens of thousands of Hindus; he destroyed temples and carried away

Under the Chola dynasty, people who worshipped Shiva came to think of him as a performer who kept the world going through his beautiful dancing and who would bring it to an end when he stopped to rest. The end was not permanent, however, as Brahma could create a new world and the cycle would continue.

Mahmud, the Turkish sultan of Gazni (in today's Afghanistan) sits in splendor on his throne, protected from the sun by an umbrella and surrounded by respectful attendants. In 1004, Mahmud invaded Panjab, (in today's Pakistan). This 15th-century scroll depicts him in miniature and describes his exploits in Persian.

the best pieces. He later used them in building mosques, Islamic places of worship, at home. Yet when he died in 1030, Mahmud's control did not extend much beyond the Panjab. He was a raider rather than an empire builder, and his descendants gradually lost control of his territories.

Some of the kingdoms of the north remained untouched by Mahmud's raids. King Bhoj of Paramara, whose realm was on the southern edge of the north-central plain, was safe from the Muslim advance. Admired both as a scholar and for his construction of irrigation works that greatly improved the agriculture of his kingdom, he was also an expert in poetry, languages, archery, yoga, and medicine. A historian from a rival state acknowledged in his chronicle: "Among poets, gallant lovers, enjoyers of life, generous donors, benefactors of the virtuous, archers, and those who regarded the universal law [of Hinduism and Buddhism] as their wealth, there is none that can equal Bhoj." Other Hindu leaders kept good relations with the Islamic rulers of the northwest by being hospitable to the Muslims who lived in their kingdoms and allowing them to construct mosques and Muslim religious schools.

Muslim military and political pressure in India led some Hindus to consider converting to Islam. Many were attracted by the clarity and simplicity of Islam's message of submission to God, and its emphasis on justice and equality within the community of believers. But most common people remained Hindus, while Muslims whose ancestors had come from elsewhere ruled much of India.

A century and a half after the death of Mahmud of Gazni, another Muslim leader conquered the Panjab again. Muhammad Ghori, whose brother was the sultan (an Arabic word meaning "ruler") of Ghur in eastern Persia, became governor of Afghanistan in 1173. From there, he launched a series of invasions of India a few years later. The most important battle took place in 1192, not far from King Harsha's old capital city. An early 19th-century Muslim historian described Muhammad's victory in his *History of the Rise of Mohammedan Power in India*: "Making one desperate charge, [his horsemen] carried death and destruction through the Hindu ranks." The invaders killed 100,000 Indian troops in what some have called the most decisive battle in the history of India.

Within a few years Muhammad's forces took Delhi, an important town on the Jamuna River, and conquered much of the rest of northern India. In 1202, Muhammad succeeded his brother as sultan of Ghur, but he was killed in Panjab four years later, without ever ruling his new Indian empire. His general Qutb-ud-Din Aybak, who began his career as a slave, was appointed the first sultan of Delhi in that same year, 1206. A new era in the history of India had begun.

CHAPTER 4

TRADE IF BY LAND AND TRADE IF BY SEA

MERCHANTS, RELIGION, AND IDEAS

In 629 the monk Xuanzang left China to go to India to visit Buddhist holy places and study at Buddhist temples. He walked all the way to India along the Silk Road. Getting there took him more than a year. He was not in a rush, and often stopped to visit temples along the way and to rest in oasis towns, communities built around sources of water in the desert. Even if he had hurried, the journey would have taken months. The trip was often dangerous and frightening. As he told a fellow monk when he returned home, at night he was "frightened by lights lit by wicked spirits and in the daytime by terrible sandstorms." Travel on the Silk Road took nerve and determination.

Today, when an airplane can travel from one end of Asia to the other in a few hours, it is hard to imagine that centuries ago the only way to make the same trip was to walk. It is even harder to imagine that anyone ever did it. But ever since the second century BCE, when the Chinese emperor Wu and

This clay statuette of a camel ridden by a bearded Central Asian man was buried in a wealthy person's tomb. Camels and skilled camel drivers were essential to travel on the Silk Road, which ran through long stretches of difficult desert country.

his resourceful explorer Zhang Qian created the Silk Road, people walked its trails that connected China, India, and the Middle East.

CAMELS AND SILK

The term "Silk Road" is a bit misleading. It is more of a path than a road, and not just one path but a network of paths leading from one town to another, each town usually located around an oasis. The traveler faced a choice of direction every time one path split into two. Some routes led toward India, some toward Persia, Syria, and the eastern Mediterranean. Camels were used to carry the silk and other goods, as well as food and water for the people. Travel was dangerous, and the services of a knowledgeable local guide were essential. Even with help, caravans sometimes were attacked by bandits, or lost the trail so the people and their animals died of thirst or starvation. The lure of profit and adventure

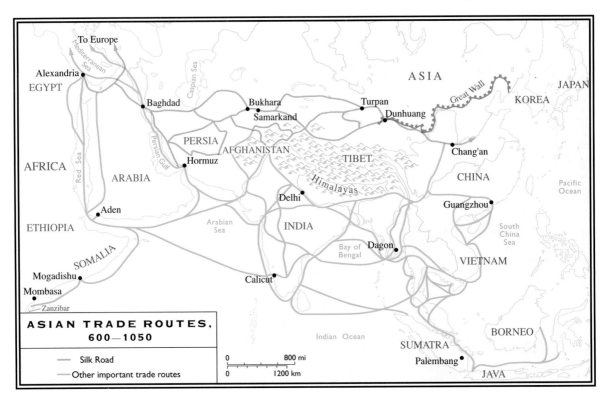

ASIAN TRADE ROUTES, 600—1050

—— Silk Road
—— Other important trade routes

0   800 mi
0   1200 km

meant that many people continued to travel along the Silk Road's various routes despite the obvious dangers.

During the Tang dynasty, when Xuanzang made his journey to India, trade along the Silk Road was booming, and there were many caravans traveling in all directions every year. Most travelers did not go as far as Xuanzang did. Most Silk Road merchants relied on what is called "down-the-line trade," which allows things to travel much farther than people. How does it work? Suppose you were a merchant in the Chinese city of Chang'an with some rolls of silk to sell. You might go with a camel caravan as far as Dunhuang, an oasis town on the eastern edge of Central Asia, and sell your silk there. You could rest for a while in Dunhuang, stay at an inn, see old friends, hear news of the caravan trade, and enjoy eating grapes, melons, and other local fruits. You might visit some of the town's many Buddhist shrines, and then take your profit and go home. Meanwhile, the merchant who bought your silk might take it as far as Turpan, several hundred miles to the west, and sell it there. Another merchant might buy it there and take it farther, and so on. In that way, your silk might go all the way from China to Baghdad, in Iraq, without any one merchant going too far from home. Along the way, your silk would have become very expensive, because each time it was sold and bought again, a certain amount was added to the price so each merchant could make a profit.

Ideas and information also traveled on the Silk Road. For example, the secret of how to raise silkworms, spin silk thread, and weave silk cloth was carried to the west, perhaps by Syrian Christian monks returning from a trip to China. Silk was being produced in the Middle East by the mid-sixth century CE. Like silk, paper was also invented in China, probably as early as the second century BCE. China exported paper as well as silk to western Asia, and the technology of

These rolls of silk fabric, found along the Silk Road, are more than 1,600 years old. Chinese farm women produced silk cloth in rolls of standard size and quality that were used to pay land taxes; the Chinese government then exported some of the silk to Central Asian lands to buy war horses and other things needed in China.

*If you want to be sure to become famous,
Let the merchant have just payment for his goods.
If you want to create a good name for yourself, Your Majesty,
Treat the caravan people well.*

—Yusuf Has Hajip, chancellor of the Uighur (a Turkish-speaking people) kingdom of Kashgar, in Central Asia, in *The Knowledge Befitting a Ruler*, 1070 papermaking eventually followed. The expansion of Islam created a big demand for a strong, inexpensive, and durable writing material to produce copies of the Quran, the Islamic holy book. Paper proved to be just right for that purpose. As an 11th-century Arab writer said in his *Book of Curious and Entertaining Information,* "paper...looks better and is more supple, more easily handled, and more convenient for writing than papyrus and parchment." By the mid-eighth century, paper was being made in the Central Asian city of Samarkand, and soon after that manufacturers established a papermaking industry in Baghdad, in present-day Iraq.

Ibn Sina, known in medieval Europe as Avicenna, knew firsthand how well ideas and information could travel along the Silk Road. He was born in the Central Asian city of Bukhara, an important stop along the Silk Road. He studied medicine as a young man, and eventually gained a reputation as the greatest Islamic doctor, mathematician, and philosopher of his time. His training as a doctor was based on ancient Greek medical works that traveled to Central Asia along the Silk Road, and his medical theories traveled to Europe, where they influenced medicine for several centuries after his death. He visited the royal library of Bukhara in 997, when he was only 17 years old. He later recalled, "I found there many rooms filled with books which were arranged in cases, row upon row....I inspected the catalogue of ancient Greek authors; I saw in this collection books of which few people have heard even the names, and which I myself have never seen either before or since."

Perhaps most important of all, the Silk Road helped spread religious ideas. In the early centuries of the Silk Road trade, many of the Central Asian mer-

A page from an Arabic translation of a medical textbook by the ancient Greek physician Dioscorides shows workers preparing honey for use as medicine. Greek scientific texts translated into Arabic were often kept in libraries in the Islamic world, not only in Arab states but also in Central Asia and India.

chants and caravan workers were Buddhists. They often prayed to Buddha for a safe journey, and wanted to make offerings to a temple at the end of a successful trip. Large Buddhist temples were established in many towns along the way, such as at Dunhuang, where artist-monks enlarged natural caves and filled them with Buddhist wall paintings and sculptures. Other religions traveled the Silk Road, too. The writing on a stone tablet in the city of Chang'an, dated 781, tells about the activities of a Syrian Christian missionary named Alopun in China during the Tang dynasty:

A brick watchtower stands alongside the Silk Road near Dunhuang, in western China. Soldiers stationed in such watchtowers, built in the Tang dynasty during the eighth century, guarded the Silk Road to keep it safe from bandits and invaders.

> When the pure bright Illustrious religion
>   [Christianity]
> Was introduced into our Tang dynasty,
> The Scriptures were translated and churches built.

A WATERY ROAD

Trade along the Silk Road allowed objects and ideas to travel the whole width of Asia and Europe, from Japan and Korea to Italy and Spain. But the Silk Road was not the only way to transport goods from one end of Asia to the other. Like the network of trails that made up the Silk Road, there was a network of shipping routes that connected the Mediterranean world, India, China, and the mainland and islands of Southeast Asia. Each route was an alternative to the other. When wars or bandits made the Silk Road more dangerous, more people used the ocean routes. When piracy became a problem on the seas, people relied on the overland caravan routes.

*W*hen the ship's people... have gone on shore, it is cus-tomary... to offer to the king daily gifts of Chinese food and wine; it is for this reason that when vessels go to Borneo they must take with them one or two good cooks.

—Zhao Rugua, Chinese maritime official, in his book *Records of Foreign Places*, about 1300

Traders also responded to changes in technology. Chinese ocean trade increased considerably beginning in the 12th century because of improvements in shipbuilding and navigational instruments, especially the magnetic compass. Around the same time, the Chinese improved the technology for making porcelain, and porcelain became a major item of international trade. The Chinese produced millions of pieces for export and shipped them to places as far away as East Africa.

Trade in the Indian Ocean began in ancient times. The Han dynasty historian Ban Gu, writing in the first century CE, described how ships left southern China "to trade for brilliant pearls, glass, strange gems and other exotic products, giving in exchange gold and silk." Around 70 CE, the Roman geographer Pliny the Elder complained that trade with India, Arabia, and China was costing the Roman Empire millions of gold coins every year because Rome bought more from the eastern lands than it sold to them. He apparently was right; thousands of ancient Roman coins have been found on the beaches of western India. This trade across the Indian Ocean that began in the time of the Roman Empire continued during later ages. As with the Silk Road, goods often traveled much farther than individual ships and merchants did.

Ships from the Red Sea and the Persian Gulf regularly sailed to India carrying gold and silver coins, and glassware and other valuable goods. The Arab and Persian merchants wanted to buy spices, such as black pepper and cinnamon from India and cloves and nutmeg from the Moluccas Islands, in what is now Indonesia. They also traded for aromatic sandalwood from India and Southeast Asia, used to make incense as well as various small wooden objects. They traded with the Chinese for silk and ceramics. One interesting item of trade was peacocks from India, which rich Europeans liked to have in their gardens.

The trading ships also carried invisible cargo such as new technologies, religious beliefs, kinds of music, and information about distant places. When Chinese merchants sailed to the tropical south to trade silk and porcelain for spices, sandalwood, rhinoceros horn, dried sea slugs (a popular ingredient in Chinese soups), pearls, and precious stones, they brought ideas with them and took new ideas home.

Trade in the Indian Ocean depended on the monsoons, seasonal winds that blow strongly in one direction or another at different times of the year. In the western Indian Ocean, the late summer monsoon blows from west to east. Ships from Arabia used these winds to sail to India in the late summer or early fall. (This monsoon also brings moist air from the Arabian Sea to the Indian subcontinent, providing the seasonal heavy rains on which Indian agriculture depends.) The ships would return to Arabia again a few months later, when the winter monsoon blew from east to west. In the eastern Indian Ocean and the South China Sea, monsoon winds also created seasonal trade, but at different times of the year.

Chinese ships sailed regularly to Vietnam, to the islands that are now the Philippines, and south to the northern coast of Borneo, an island southwest of the Philippines. Ships from India dominated trade in regions farther to the west. Many Indian merchants and sailors spent part of every year in Southeast Asian port towns. Suppose you were an

An Indonesian sailing ship is carved on a wall of the Temple of Borobudur. Ships like this one sailed throughout the Indian Ocean and the South China Sea, carrying trade goods that might have come from as far away as China, India, or the Middle East.

[Sumatra] was verdant and beautiful, most of its trees being coco-palms, . . . clove trees, . . . mangos, . . . sweet orange trees, and camphor-canes.

—Ibn Battuta, Arab traveler, about an island that is part of present-day Indonesia, in *Travels,* 1347

Indian merchant who had brought a cargo of cotton cloth to the island of Java, in what is now Indonesia, to exchange for cloves and other spices. As you would have to stay in Java for several months waiting for the monsoon, you would want a familiar inn to live in, and restaurants serving Indian food, and a temple where you could worship. Permanent settlements of Indians soon sprang up in Southeast Asian port towns to provide visitors with the comforts of home, and also to manage local trade. Local people in the port towns were curious about the religions of the Indian Buddhist monks and Hindu priests. Many Southeast Asian people, not only merchants but members of the ruling class as well, accepted Buddhism or Hinduism, in addition to their own beliefs in many gods of nature. The Indians themselves put down local roots. Few Indian women traveled abroad, so many of the Indian merchants in Southeast Asia married local women, strengthening their ties to their adopted homeland.

HINDU AND BUDDHIST KINGDOMS

New states, heavily influenced by India, were founded in Southeast Asia specifically in response to ocean trade. At the beginning of the eighth century a kingdom called Sailendra was founded on the island of Java. The people of Sailendra quickly became wealthy from rice agriculture, and the kingdom became a major center of trade. Sailendra was a Buddhist kingdom, and it is best remembered today for building the Temple of Borobudur. The temple is a huge and impressive structure, more like an artificial mountain than a building. It consists of nine sculptured stone terraces, in the form of a mandala or magical diagram; the temple is a model of the universe in miniature. Its stone walls are carved with scenes from Buddhist stories, and on top of the temple are many statues of the Buddha, each in an individual bell-shaped shrine.

In the ninth century, the power of Sailendra declined, and it was succeeded by another Javanese kingdom called Mataram. Its rulers embraced Hinduism rather than Buddhism, and built a large Hindu temple at Prambanan, not far from Borobudur. The kingdom of Mataram reached the height of its power in the 11th century, under King Airlangga. His policies were good for ordinary working people, as well as aristocrats and rich merchants. He created new water-control and irrigation systems to increase the production of rice. His engineers deepened the channels of the kingdom's main seaport, which led to more ocean trade. He also protected and promoted local Javanese culture; his

The Buddhist Temple of Borobudur, on the island of Java (in today's Indonesia) was built around 800 CE. The temple is in the form of a mandala, a model of the universe. It has four circular terraces on top of five square terraces, representing different levels of heaven and earth.

The circular terraces of the Temple of Borobudur are ringed with statues of the Buddha enclosed within bell-shaped domes. Visitors to the temple could reach into the domes to touch the statues; they believed that doing so could make wishes come true.

large and beautifully decorated palace became a center of Javanese art, music, theater, and dance. Airlangga was a Hindu, and he regarded himself as a human incarnation, or living human example, of the Hindu god Vishnu, the sustainer of the world. In 1045, four years before his death, he retired to live a life of simplicity and religious devotion. When he died, his tomb was decorated with a sculpture of him in the form of Vishnu riding on the back of Garuda, a giant magical bird that serves as the messenger of the Hindu gods.

By Airlangga's time, however, the Hindu period of Southeast Asian history was coming to an end. Islam was already making its presence felt in his island empire, as Arab and Persian merchants living in the kingdom began to build mosques and schools for their own communities. Just as in India at the same time, Islam was about to transform the nature of religious belief and political power in the islands of Southeast Asia.

The Far West

BUREAU OF HISTORY, HISTORY OF THE TANG DYNASTY, MID-10TH CENTURY

Chinese people during the Tang dynasty were very open to foreign goods and ideas, and interested in learning about other countries. The History of the Tang Dynasty, *written by a group of officials, contains descriptions of many foreign lands, including this account of the Byzantine (Eastern Roman) Empire—the far West, from China's point of view. Clearly based on eyewitness information, it gives a fairly accurate picture of the Byzantine Empire, although the poison-sniffing bird sounds like a folktale. This account shows how effectively information could travel on the Silk Road, even over distances of thousands of miles.*

The country of Fulin [Byzantium], also called Daqin [Roman Syria], is located above the western sea [Indian Ocean]. In the southeast it borders on Bosi [Persia] ... There are four hundred cities, and inhabited places are close together. The eaves, pillars, and window-bars of their palaces are frequently made with crystal and opaque glass.

There are twelve high ministers who together are in charge of government matters. [When the king leaves the palace,] a man with a bag follows the king's carriage. Any person who has a complaint can throw a written statement into the bag. When the king comes back to the palace he decides the right and wrong of each one. Their kings are not permanent rulers, but are selected on the basis of merit. If an unusual disaster occurs in the country, or if wind and rain come at the wrong time, the king is removed and another man is put in his place. The king's cap is shaped like a bird raising its wings; its trimmings are beset with precious pearls; he wears silk-embroidered clothing, ... He sits on a throne with golden ornaments. He has a bird like a goose; its feathers are green, and it always sits on a cushion by the side of the king. Whenever anything poisonous has been put into the king's meals, the bird will crow. The walls of their capital are built of granite, and are of enormous height. The city [Constantinople, now called Istanbul] contains in all over 100,000 households. ... The country contains much gold, silver, and rare gems. ... All the valuable curiosities of the West are exported from this country.

CHAPTER 5

BONES AND BUDDHISTS
EARLY KOREA AND JAPAN

In 514 CE, Kim Wonjong proclaimed himself king of Silla, a state that controlled the eastern part of the Korean peninsula. In 535 he made Buddhism the official religion of Silla. This strengthened Korea's ties with China, and also led to increased Korean influence in Japan. The king also classified his kingdom's aristocracy according to "bone ranks." (The word "bone" in Korea expressed an idea similar to "blood" in Europe. For example, a European aristocrat was said to have "noble blood.") He created different bone-rank titles to indicate people's status in society. He and his family were "hallowed bone aristocrats," while his wife's

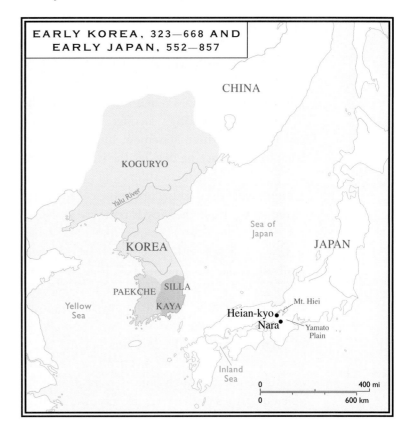

EARLY KOREA, 323—668 AND
EARLY JAPAN, 552—857

CHINA

KOGURYO

Yalu River

Sea of
Japan

JAPAN

KOREA

PAEKCHE SILLA
KAYA

Yellow
Sea

Mt. Hiei
Heian-kyo
Nara
Yamato
Plain

Inland
Sea

0   400 mi
0   600 km

family and some other noble families had the lower rank of "true bone aristocrats." Below them, other nobles got other bone ranks, and the king issued regulations about what kinds of houses and carriages they were allowed to have and what kinds of clothing they were allowed to wear. The aristocracy was only the smallest top layer of society. The vast majority of people were commoners, including landowners, merchants, tenant farmers, and slaves.

Originally decorated with semi-precious stones, this gold crown is typical of crowns worn by the kings of Silla, Paekche, and Koguryo, three states that shared authority over the Korean peninsula in the sixth century. Korean rulers began calling themselves by the Chinese word for "king," and they made efforts to develop stronger and more centralized governments. Elaborate gold crowns thus symbolize the expansion of royal authority in Korea.

In Silla, as in China, the throne was normally passed from father to son. Unlike China, where women rulers were regarded as unnatural, in Korea it was quite possible for a woman to rule. When a Silla king died in 632 leaving no son as his heir, his daughter Tongman, known after her death as Queen Sondok, inherited the throne and ruled successfully for 15 years.

As queen, Sondok formed a strong alliance with China's Tang dynasty and enjoyed a friendship with Emperor Tang Taizong. As the the 13th-century monk Iryon wrote in *Samguk yusa* (Memorabilia of the Three Kingdoms), once the emperor sent her a painting of some flowers. She said to her advisors, "The flowers are pretty, but they have no smell." Her advisors asked how she could tell that from a painting. Queen Sondok replied, "If the flowers had a sweet smell, the painting would show bees and butterflies flying near them."

Queen Sondok also built an observatory for studying the planets and stars. This tall stone tower still exists today and is one of the oldest such structures in the world. Officials used it to study the movements of the stars and planets, to observe eclipses of the sun and the moon, and to watch for anything strange or unexpected in the night sky. Confucian theory said that good government was reflected in the movements of the heavens. If all the heavenly bodies

This earthenware vessel in the shape of a Silla warrior on horseback had both practical and religious functions. It could be used to pour lamp oil from the cup on the horse's rump or to pour water from the horse's stomach. It symbolized the transport of the soul to the other world through land, of which it was made, and water, which it contained.

stayed in their proper patterns, it meant that the ruler was virtuous, but unusual phenomena such as comets were taken to be warnings that something was wrong in the world.

For a long time, Silla had competed for control of the Korean peninsula with two other important states, Koguryo in the northwest and Paekche in the southwest. In the seventh century, Silla's leaders used military force and diplomacy to defeat these two rivals and unify most of the Korean peninsula. Silla maintained very close relations with China and sent missions bearing Korean products to the Tang capital. Many Korean Buddhist monks went to China to study, and some traveled as far as India to visit the homeland of the Buddha. Korean Confucian scholars also visited China; some passed the civil service examinations there and became officials in the Tang government. Korea enjoyed peace and prosperity during the following century and a half.

Silla power began to decline during the ninth century. Disputes about who should inherit the throne weakened royal authority. Corrupt officials made huge fortunes, while the common people suffered from higher rents and higher taxes. Poor families were forced to sell members into slavery to earn money to pay their rents, taxes, and debts. A series of popular uprisings showed that the common people were desperate for relief from their burdens. Finally, in 935, Wang Kon, a wealthy farmer who had become a rebel leader, accepted the surrender of the last Silla king. Wang

Serve your sovereign with loyalty; attend your parents with filial piety; treat your friends with sincerity; do not retreat from a battlefield; be discriminating about the taking of life.

—Korean Buddhist monk Wongwang, in his essay "Five Principles," 608

Kon proclaimed himself king of a new state that he called Koryo. His Koryo dynasty ruled most of the peninsula for the next 450 years, giving us the name "Korea."

PRINCE SHOTOKU CHANGES THE RULES

In 552 the king of Paekche in Korea sent a statue of the Buddha to the king of Japan, along with some monks to explain what Buddhism was about. Some of Japan's powerful military clans were interested in the new religion, but others opposed it. They were afraid that the gods of Japan's own ancient religion, Shinto, which means the "way of the gods," would be offended by the Buddhist statue. But once Buddhism and other Chinese and Korean ideas began to flow into Japan from Korea, it was hard to stop them.

In 587, a young woman named Suiko was made queen of Japan by her uncle, the head of the dominant Soga clan. Worried that her power might be challenged, the uncle also appointed a prince to serve as co-ruler with her. Prince Shotoku, as the co-ruler was known, proved to be a very gifted and capable young man. He eagerly absorbed as much as he could of the new ideas of Buddhism and Confucianism that were coming to Japan from Korea. In 604, he issued a 17-article constitution that transformed the nature of kingship and government in Japan.

Prince Shotoku's constitution was based on a mixture of Confucian and Buddhist ideas. The first article, in Confucian style, emphasized the importance of cooperation in government. The second urged reverence for the Three Treasures of Buddhism: Buddha, the teachings of Buddhism, and the religious community of Buddhist monks. Other articles required officials to follow Confucian standards of conduct and to avoid oppressing the common people. The constitution makes it clear that the ruler is the supreme power in the land: "In a country there are not two lords, the people have not two masters."

Prince Shotoku's aim in writing this constitution was to establish the ruler of Japan as a true emperor, like the emperor of China. He claimed that the ruler alone, and not

The Buddha Amitabha is the ruler of the Pure Land in the Western Paradise. He stands on a pedestal shaped like a lotus, a beautiful flower that grows out of mud, just as the enlightened person can rise from the impure everyday world. He raises his right hand as if to reassure people that anyone who calls out his name can be saved.

the nobles, had the right to collect taxes from landowners. In 646, powerful aristocrats allied with the imperial court introduced the Taika ("Great Transformation") reforms. These measures gave more power to the emperor and strengthened Prince Shotoku's earlier claim that the ruler owned everything: "From this time forward the sale of land is not allowed."

The reforms also established a system of Chinese-style civil service exams, but it was less extensive than in China. The nobles refused to accept the idea that they would have to compete with commoners for government jobs, and the highest positions continued to be reserved for aristocrats. And many aristocratic officials just collected their salaries without doing any work. Like Korea, Japan was strongly influenced by Chinese culture and political ideas, but not all the new ideas from China took hold.

Prince Shotoku demonstrated his commitment to Buddhism by building a beautiful temple near the Yamato Plain of central Japan. Called the Horyuji, the temple included a five-story pagoda tower in the latest Chinese style. (Some of the original buildings of this temple still exist today; they are the oldest wooden buildings in the world.) In 710, the Japanese court moved to a new capital city, Nara, which was built not far from Prince Shotoku's temple.

Haniwa, hollow ceramic sculptures of farmers, women, horses, and warriors, encircled large burial mounds and stood watch over the dead in sixth-century Japan. This warrior wears a helmet, bears a sword, and stands at attention, suggesting the existence of strict military discipline in Japan long before the rise of the samurai class and its code of Bushido (the "way of the warrior").

If a Chinese visitor to the new capital had approached Nara along the country road leading northward to the city, he would have been surprised to see that Nara was not surrounded by a defensive wall. At the city's edge the road just suddenly widened to become the capital's main avenue. The Chinese visitor, thinking about this, would have realized that unlike his own country, the island of Japan had no neighbors threatening to invade. But in other ways the Chinese visitor would have found Nara very familiar. Like the Tang

Prince Shotoku, who governed Yamato Japan as regent to his Aunt Suiko, is accompanied by his two children in this seventh-century portrait. Shotoku built up the authority of the Japanese emperor without claiming that authority for himself, and his children would not inherit his position as regent. From their hairstyles and dress, it might be hard to tell whether Shotoku's children were girls or boys, but their swords indicate that they are male.

capital of Chang'an, its streets ran north-south and east-west in a grid pattern. The royal palace was located in the northern part of the city, facing south. Walking along the main avenue, the visitor would have been impressed by the Chinese-style architecture of Buddhist temples and the palaces of aristocrats. The smell of incense and the sound of monks chanting in the temples would have made the visitor feel right at home.

In addition to religious ideas and architectural styles, one of the most important things that Japan adopted from China was writing. The Chinese and Japanese languages are

The Chinese monk Kuiji traveled to Japan in the seventh century and brought with him the Faxiang school of Buddhism, which taught that the world we see and touch is only an illusion. This 14th-century portrait of Kuiji shows his distinctive bushy eyebrows.

very different from each other in structure and grammar, however. The thousands of Chinese characters, one for each separate word, are not very easily adapted to the Japanese language. The Japanese dealt with the problem in two ways. Some people simply learned Chinese and used it as their written language. This worked because all the Confucian classics, Buddhist scriptures, and other important books that were imported into Japan were written in Chinese. The second, more awkward, solution was to use Chinese characters only for sound, but not for meaning, and to write the Japanese language phonetically. In the early Nara period, poetry, history, and other works in the Japanese language began to be written down in that way.

Emperors and wealthy aristocrats competed with each other to give money and materials to build Buddhist temples at Nara. One temple was built to hold a 53-foot-tall bronze statue of Vairocana, the Buddha of Universal Wisdom. The temples attracted thousands of monks and grew large and powerful, threatening the authority of the imperial government. Relations between the court and the temples came to a crisis under the female ruler Empress Koken. She was a very strong leader, but she created a scandal by becoming romantically involved with the head monk of one of Nara's temples. Alarmed that the throne had almost fallen into the hands of a commoner monk, powerful families at court decided in 784 to move the capital away from Nara.

A GOLDEN AGE FOR THE UPPER CRUST

In 795, after a decade living in temporary locations, the court finally established itself in the new capital of Heian-kyo, which means "capital of peace and tranquility" and is modern-day Kyoto. Like Nara, the city was a smaller version of the Tang capital at Chang'an, built on a grid pattern with the imperial palace in the north. To the northeast of the city was a large mountain, Mount Hiei. In Japanese belief, northeast is an unlucky direction, so a large Buddhist temple was built on top of the mountain to protect the capital from evil spirits. Buddhism remained strong during the Heian period, and many Japanese monks traveled to China to study and bring back new information about Buddhism. But the temples did not dominate the new capital as they had at Nara.

The emperor also lost some of his power. In the city of Heian-kyo, a system of government evolved in which the emperor was supposedly the supreme ruler, but in fact he shared power with the main aristocratic families, especially the Fujiwara family. The Fujiwaras had led the Taika reforms, opposed the power of the Buddhist temples in Nara, and favored the move to Heian-kyo. In the new capital, they supplied most of the emperors' wives, which kept the Fujiwaras in power. They gradually were able to require each successive emperor to marry a Fujiwara daughter when he was about 12 years old, have sons very early, and then retire. (Emperors could also have many concubines, or minor wives.) This meant that the emperor was almost always a child or teenager, which left the real authority entirely in the hands of the Fujiwara regent who acted in the emperor's name.

Fujiwara Michinaga, for example, held the title of regent for only two years, but by producing several intelligent and attractive daughters and managing his own family well he effectively ruled Japan for 30 years, until 1027. Michinaga was the father-in-law of two emperors, grandfather of a third, grandfather and great-grandfather of a fourth, and grandfather and father-in-law of a fifth. As he boasted in a poem:

> This world, I think,
> Is indeed my world.
> Like the full moon I shine,
> Uncovered by any cloud.

During the early 11th century, the great majority of Japan's 5 million people were poor and downtrodden farmers. Smaller numbers were merchants, urban craft workers, and servants in the households of the rich. The tiny Heian aristocracy, about 1 percent of the population, enjoyed a golden age at the expense of everyone else. Almost all of them lived in Heian-kyo, the center of social, artistic and intellectual life. Their agricultural estates in the countryside, run by managers, produced wealth that flowed to the capital. Luxury objects of all kinds—such as beautifully woven and embroidered silk robes, porcelain and lacquer tableware, and musical instruments inlaid with rare woods and mother-of-pearl—were produced in Japan and also imported from Korea, China, and the countries along the Silk Road. But the Heian love of beauty was often touched with sadness, reflecting the Buddhist idea that life is really an illusion held together by desire. A key idea of Heian art and literature is *mono no aware*, which means "the fragility of things." This was reflected in a favorite aristocratic activity, viewing cherry blossoms in the spring. People at blossom-viewing parties felt that the flowers were all the more lovely because of how quickly they would fade.

By the 11th century, Japanese scholars had worked out a new and useful writing system. It combined Chinese characters, used to write nouns and verbs, with simple symbols, used to write the syllables needed to express Japanese grammar. Men were still expected to learn Chinese, which was used for important official documents. Women were free to use the newly developing and distinctively Japanese writing system to create more popular forms of literature, such as diaries, travelogues, and novels. By the standards of most societies of that era, aristocratic women in Heian Japan enjoyed a great deal of personal freedom, and this was reflected in their writing.

Nothing can be worse than allowing the driver of one's ox-carriage to be badly dressed.

—Sei Shonagon, Heian period court lady, writer, and snob, from her memoir *The Pillow Book*, about 1030

This 18th-century scroll depicts a scene from The Tale of Genji. *While Prince Genji's new wife watches a game of kickball from behind a bamboo screen, her cat rushes out, briefly revealing her to Kashiwagi, Genji's rival at court.*

The outstanding woman writer in the Heian period—perhaps in all of Japanese history—was Murasaki Shikibu. Murasaki was the pen name of a woman born into a minor branch of the Fujiwara family. Quiet and well educated, in 1005 she became a companion to one of Michinaga's daughters, who was married to the current emperor. After the death of the ruler and the retirement of her mistress, Murasaki drew on her experience at court to write a novel called *The*

A Boy Becomes a Man

MURASAKI SHIKIBU, THE TALE OF GENJI, ABOUT 1010

Genji, the handsome prince who is the hero of Murasaki Shikibu's novel The Tale of Genji, *is based in part on the real-life aristocrat Fujiwara Michinaga. In the novel, he is an idealized figure, a model of perfect behavior as well as a master of poetry, music, and other arts. Like many aristocrats of the time, Genji was romantically involved with many women, and his love affairs make up a large part of the novel's plot. Murasaki presents him as an admirable figure, because he remained loyal to all his women friends, even when a relationship had ended. In this scene, he participates in a ceremony in which he leaves his childhood behind and symbolically becomes a man.*

His Majesty was reluctant to spoil Genji's boyish charm, but in Genji's twelfth year he gave him his coming of age, busying himself personally with the preparations and adding new embellishments to the ceremony. Lest the event seem less imposing than the one for the Heir Apparent, done some years ago in the Shishiden [Palace], and lest anything go amiss, he issued minute instructions for the banquets. . . .

He had his throne face east from the outer, eastern chamber of his residence, with the seats for the young man and his sponsor, the Minister, before him. Genji appeared at the hour of the Monkey [4:00 p.m.]. His Majesty appeared to regret that Genji would never again look as he did now, with his hair tied in twin [ponytails] and his face radiant with the freshness of youth. The Lord of the Treasury and the Chamberlain did their duty. The Lord of the Treasury was plainly sorry to cut off such beautiful hair, and His Majesty, who wished desperately that [Genji's mother] might have been there to see it, needed the greatest self-mastery not to weep.

All present shed tears when, after donning the headdress and withdrawing to the anteroom, Genji then appeared in the robes of a man and stepped down into the garden to salute his Sovereign. His Majesty, of course, was still more deeply moved, and in his mind he sadly reviewed the past, when the boy's mother had been such a comfort to him. He had feared that Genji's looks might suffer once his hair was put up, at least while he remained so young, but not at all: he only looked more devastatingly handsome than ever.

Tale of Genji, one of the first works to be written in Japanese script. Most scholars consider this to be the world's first full-length novel. It remains one of the best ever written because of the depth of its characters. After Murasaki finished the novel, she retired, and little is known about her later years.

The Fujiwara family stayed in power for another century and a half after the time of Michinaga, but their system of maintaining power eventually caused them to lose control of the imperial government. By dominating the throne indirectly through marriage and having large private estates on which they did not pay taxes, they weakened the throne and deprived the state of income. By focusing their attention on running things in the capital, they allowed other families to build up their military strength in the countryside. During the 12th century two military clans clashed in a series of civil wars that destroyed much of the capital and brought the Heian period to an end in 1185.

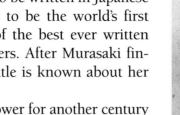

*On a spring hillside
I took lodging for the night;
and as I slept
the blossoms kept falling—
even in the midst of my
  dreams.*

—Heian poet Ki no Tsurayuki,
"Spring," about 900

A great warrior of Heian Japan, Minamoto no Yoshi'ie, pauses at Nakoso Barrier, thought to be a boundary between the civilized and uncivilized worlds, as he returns home from a successful campaign. This 18th-century hanging scroll includes one of his poems, a sign of his learning, as well as a painting of cherry blossoms, conveying the idea that the beauty of life is heightened by its brevity.

CHAPTER 6

HORSEMEN AND GENTLEMEN
THE SONG DYNASTY IN CHINA

Yelü Abaoji was chief of the Khitan people, hunters and herders who inhabited northeastern China in the 10th century. When the Tang dynasty collapsed in 907, Abaoji extended his authority south of the Great Wall. Abaoji was an expert horseman and archer who was at home on the grasslands and forests of the northeast, but he was also a good politician. He realized that ruling a large territory would take more than horsepower. Abaoji declared himself the head of a new dynasty, which he called the Liao, after a river in his homeland. He established two governments: one made of military men to rule the Khitan people of the steppe and one made of civilians to govern the Chinese people in agricultural regions within the Great Wall. According to the

This detail from a 12th-century scroll entitled Going up the River on the Qingming Festival *depicts the busy streets of the Song capital city of Kaifeng before its fall to the Jurchen Jin state. Shops and restaurants conducted business both night and day in most parts of the city, and goods were brought from Central Asia on camels as well as by horseback.*

THE NORTHERN SONG
DYNASTY, 960—1126

LIAO

XIXIA

Yanjing •

Huang He (Yellow River)

Yellow
Sea

• Kaifeng

NORTHERN
SONG

Huai River

Yangzi River

0   400 mi

0   600 km

South China
Sea

memoir of an ambassador from the central plain who visited
him in 926, Abaoji remarked, "I can speak Chinese, but I
never speak it in the presence of my people because I fear
that they may emulate the Chinese and grow soft and timid."

In 960 a rebel Chinese military officer named Zhao
Kuangyin conquered the part of China that the Liao
dynasty did not control, and established his own dynasty,
which he called the Song. Zhao kept his armed forces under
tight control; established his capital at Kaifeng, a city on the
south bank of the Huang He (Yellow River); and appointed
civil officials to govern the entire country. The Song rulers
relied on diplomacy and payments to maintain an uneasy
peace on their borders. They agreed to supply the Liao
rulers with 200,000 bolts of silk and 100,000 ounces of silver every year, in return for which the Liao promised not to
attack. The Song also tried to win the goodwill of the Liao
by arranging for a certain number of well-born young
Chinese women to be sent north to become wives of the
Liao emperor and his high officials.

In 1038 the Tangut people in northwestern China (relatives of the Tibetans) set up a dynasty called the Xixia. In 1044 the Song officials agreed to send large annual donations of silk, silver, and tea to the Xixia rulers to preserve the peace. Like Abaoji, the Tangut chieftain was a tough nomad who worried about his people being influenced by what he considered the "softness" of China. He even criticized his own father for wearing silk. According to his biography in the official history of the Song dynasty, he once said, "To dress in skins and furs and to tend one's flocks and herds are... suited to the Tangut nature. A bold leader's life should be that of a king or a conqueror. What does that have to do with brocades and fine silks?"

THIS TEST *REALLY* COUNTS

In contrast to their northern neighbors, the Song dynasty emphasized diplomacy and civilian government, which gave new power to the scholar-official class. Government officials from prosperous landowning families used wealth, education, and their official positions together with family connections and friendship to keep themselves in the top layer of society. At the same time, there was a growing feeling among Song subjects that public service was an obligation for well-educated people.

The examination system, which reached a new peak of importance during the Song dynasty, helped create this new class of scholar-officials. Exams were held every three years at the county, prefecture (a unit of several counties, similar to an American state), and national level. Only 10 percent of the candidates who took the test were allowed to pass at each level. On the other hand, some passing grades were reserved for each county and prefecture, so there would be successful candidates from most parts of the country. In practice, no one could hope to pass the exams without a thorough education. Successful candidates were almost always from families wealthy enough to afford books, schools, and private tutors for their sons.

Suppose you were the son of a wealthy family in Song China. Your formal education would begin at around age

The world today is the same as the world of the ancient kings. There were many capable men in those times. Why are there so few today? It is because we do not train and cultivate men in the proper way.

—Wang Anshi, reform-minded official, "Memorial to Emperor Renzong," fourth emperor of the Song dynasty, about 1070

Song Renzong, the ruler of China during the late 11th century, sits at a table and examines essays submitted by scholars taking the civil service examination. Song rulers took their jobs as chief examiners seriously, and the Song drew more officials from the ranks of scholars who passed the examinations than any previous rulers of China. This watercolor on silk was painted in the 18th century, when rulers also relied heavily on the examinations to recruit officials.

five. Most likely your family would hire a private tutor for you; you might study with a small group of brothers and cousins. For about the first eight to ten years, your lessons would involve memorizing the main Confucian classics—works of philosophy, history, and literature. You would also spend many hours with brush, ink, and paper practicing writing thousands of Chinese characters perfectly. This was essential, because on the official exams, any paper written in bad handwriting would automatically get a failing grade. At last, in your early teens, the tutor would begin teaching you the meaning of the books you had memorized, so you would be prepared to answer examination questions about them.

The examinations were deliberately difficult. An exam question might ask you to explain the meaning of these lines from the Confucian *Classic of Poetry*: "Stalwart was Duke Liu/Not one to sit down or relax." To answer the question, you would have to know that these lines were from an

The Art of Bamboo

SU SHI, "ESSAY ON THE BAMBOO PAINTINGS OF WEN TONG," ABOUT 1070

Su Shi, also known by his pen name Su Dongpo, came close to the ideal Song scholar-official, a person of practical accomplishments who also had a deep understanding of the arts. He is now best known as a poet, but he was also an important art critic whose ideas about painting were highly respected by his contemporaries. In an essay on the work of his teacher Wen Tong, who specialized in painting bamboo, Su Shi makes it clear that he values art not only as a skillful representation of nature, but also as a source of moral inspiration, such as a scholar's ability to bend, and not break, in the face of oppression.

In "Branch of Bamboo," the Song painter Wen Tong manages to capture the essential nature of the plant, while at the same time expressing his own ideas and feelings. Chinese artists saw art as more than just painting pictures; they also used it as a way of illustrating moral ideals.

When bamboo first grow, they are sprouts only an inch long, yet all their joints and leaves are already complete. They pass from shedding their sheaths, like cicada husks and snakeskins, and reach a point when they thrust up like swords ten yards high: this occurs as something innate within them. Nowadays painters do them joint by joint and accumulate their foliage leaf by leaf—and there is nothing left of a bamboo in it! The reason is that in order to paint bamboo, the painter must get the bamboo beforehand in his heart; then, when he takes hold of the brush and looks fully, he actually sees what he wants to paint and quickly sets out in its pursuit, and it is completed with a flourish of the brush, in which he goes after what he has seen like a falcon swooping down on a bounding hare—if you go off just a little, it gets away. This is what Wen Tong taught me. I could not do this, yet I recognized that it was true. When the mind has recognized how something is true, yet is unable to do it, the internal and the external are not the same; mind and hand do not respond to one another, which is an error of inadequate learning. . . . This goes beyond the question of bamboo.

ancient poem about a nobleman who made a risky trip to the northern grasslands. You also had to explain what these lines meant in relation to what was happening in your own day. So your answer would be about northern frontier policy. In addition, your answer would have to be written in a particular form: an essay for one question, for example, and a poem for another. Although the system had its limitations, people at the time respected it as a reasonably fair and efficient means of selecting capable, honest officials.

At the beginning of the 12th century, the Khitan Liao dynasty—with whom the Song state maintained an uneasy peace—began to lose its grip on northern China. The Jurchen, people who came from the vast woodlands northeast of China, challenged, defeated, and replaced the Khitans. The Jurchen leaders, now calling themselves rulers of the Jin dynasty, quickly began to move southward into Song territory. The last Song emperor at the northern capital of Kaifeng, who happened to be a very good artist but a rather poor leader, offered some resistance but soon admitted defeat. In 1126 the Song government abandoned northern China.

The period of history from 1127 to the end of the Song dynasty is known as the Southern Song, because the Song capital was moved to Lin'an (present-day Hangzhou) on the southern coast of China. This was the first time in history that a seaport had been made the capital of China. Cut off from access to the Silk Road by the Jin state to their north, Chinese merchants began to expand overseas trade with the countries of Southeast Asia and the Indian Ocean.

SHIPS, ROCKETS, AND PHILOSOPHERS

The increase in ocean-going trade soon led to improvements in Chinese shipbuilding and navigation. Shipbuilders made vessels with multiple masts and sternpost rudders (a steering mechanism mounted on the rear of the ship, replacing less efficient steering oars). The magnetic compass made ocean navigation safer and more reliable, especially on cloudy nights. The Chinese made compasses by rubbing an iron needle with magnetite—a naturally occurring magnetic iron ore—to magnetize it. The needle could then be sus-pended from a silk thread or inserted in a piece of straw and floated in a bowl of water. Either method produced a useful compass, and using a compass needle to find directions caught on quickly among sea captains.

Song military engineers invented new weapons using what they called "fire powder" (that is, what Westerners would later call "gunpowder"). Fire powder had been dis-covered in the late Tang dynasty by scholars trying to invent a medicine that would make people live forever. Other inven-tors soon grasped fire powder's military potential. The Song army used it to make flame throwers by filling a bamboo tube with a mixture of gunpowder and oil. These proved very effective in defending city walls against Jurchen attackers in 1120. Song dynasty military engineers also developed bombs and explosive rockets that could be hurled long distances by catapults. But these weapons did not allow the Song to over-come their neighbors and restore the Chinese realm to the borders it had had during the Tang dynasty.

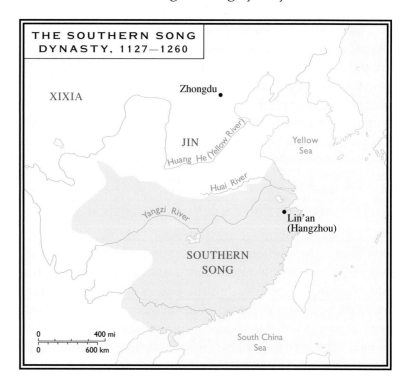

THE SOUTHERN SONG
DYNASTY, 1127—1260

Chinese farmers of the Song period transplanted rice seedlings and threshed grain by hand, and they also used water buffalo to plow the fields as their ancestors had since Han times. During the Song, farmers adopted early-ripening rice, which permitted them to grow two and sometimes three crops a year. The increase in food production helped China's population grow to 100 million for the first time.

New farming techniques allowed the Chinese to grow much more food than before. For example, in 1012 the Song Ministry of Agriculture imported seeds for early-ripening varieties of rice from Southeast Asia, and farmers quickly modified them through selective breeding—choosing plants with desired qualities—to suit Chinese conditions. Because the new rice could be harvested fewer than 120 days after planting, farmers were able to grow three crops a year (usually, two crops of rice and one of vegetables) where soil, water, and climate permitted it. Members of the landowning scholar-official class soon wrote and published agricultural manuals to spread the news of these improved rice varieties that were widely adopted by the end of the 11th century.

Other Song intellectuals devoted themselves to questions of philosophy and religion. They were inspired in part by the challenge of Buddhism, which seemed to offer a deeper understanding of the meaning of life and death than could be found in the ancient Confucian classics. Zhu Xi, who was born into a southern scholar-official family with a long tradition of public service, became the leader of a new style of classical scholarship. Zhu Xi passed the civil exams with very high grades, but after a brief official career he devoted himself to teaching and writing. Zhu rejected Buddhism and believed that Confucianism, properly under-

A sleeping child supports a headrest, implying the user should "sleep like a baby," despite the hardness of the material that passed for a Song-period pillow. These ceramic objects, made from special clay fired at a high temperature and covered with a fine glaze, were an important part of China's exports to the world. Centuries later, the smooth round surfaces reminded the Portuguese of pigs, causing them to coin the word that later became "porcelain" in English.

stood, could provide a satisfying basis for spiritual life. He borrowed from the philosophical principles of Daoism the idea of the Dao, or Way, a fundamental force that governs everything that happens in the universe.

Zhu taught that the entire visible world is a temporary reflection of an eternal, perfect pattern, and that the spiritual goal of humans should be to make their lives conform as closely as possible to that eternal perfection. He was not interested in practical policies for reforming government. As he explained to his students, who compiled a *Book of Sayings*, "Integrity always brings benefits, but benefit should not be the first thing one speaks of, nor the first thing that the heart seeks." Zhu Xi's philosophy came to be known as Neo-Confucianism, or "new Confucianism," and it set a new standard for later generations studying and applying the Confucian classics.

BIG CITIES AND SMALL FEET

As much as 20 percent of China's population lived in cities during the Song dynasty, and the capitals Kaifeng and Lin'an had populations of about 1 million. Most urban areas were bustling centers of trade and manufacturing as well as of government. Workers produced or processed large quantities of porcelain, silk cloth, tea, and other goods. City life offered pleasures for the wealthy and for ordinary citizens alike. The writer Meng Yuanlao recorded in his memoir, published in 1147, that there were 72 large restaurants and innumerable small ones to serve the people of Kaifeng. He noted that each of the city's two largest bakeries "had upwards of 50 ovens." They supplied street vendors who sold cakes and buns from before dawn to after midnight. Around the same time, the artist Zhang Zeduan painted a scroll called *Going up the River on the Qing-Ming Festival*, depicting the many shops and active street life of Kaifeng.

In an instant the waiter would be back carrying three dishes forked in his left hand, while on his right arm from hand to shoulder he carried about twenty bowls doubled up, and he distributed them precisely as everyone had ordered without an omission or a mistake.

—Meng Yuanlao, writer on city life, in his book *Dreaming of the Splendor of the Eastern Capital [Kaifeng]*, 1147

The painting gives an idealized view of the energy and diversity of life in this great city.

Many Song dynasty artists painted large landscapes dominated by towering mountains. The most admired painter of the Song period, Fan Kuan, did what many other intellectuals only talked about doing: he became a Daoist hermit living in absolute simplicity in a small cottage deep in the mountains of central China. His paintings, in which human figures appear small and insignificant, were inspired by his surroundings. A contemporary critic said about Fan Kuan's paintings that "they instantly made one feel as if one were walking along those shaded mountain paths, and even in the middle of summer one felt chilled and wanted to bundle up."

Song intellectual life stimulated a strong demand for books on many different subjects. This demand spurred enterprising merchants to develop a commercial publishing industry. For example, in the mid-11th century, the Yü family opened a bookstore in the small city of Jianyang, on the southeastern coast of China, which they soon expanded into the printing business. A century later, Yü Renzhong, a descendent of the company's founder, earned a civil service degree, which he used to develop contacts and expand the business, becoming one of the most prominent publishers of the Song period. This scholar-businessman owned a personal library of more than 10,000 volumes. His family remained in the publishing business at the same address for the next 500 years.

The rise of the scholar-official class during the Song period had mixed effects on the status of women. A few

Scholar-painters such as Fan Kuan escaped from the densely populated cities and villages of Song China and "headed for the hills." There, inspired by the Daoist idea of communing with nature, they often painted scenes like this one of scholars dwarfed by the landscapes through which they traveled.

We yearn for forests and streams because they are beautiful places. A painter should create with this thought in mind, and a beholder should study a painting with this thought in mind.

—Song landscape painter Guo Xi, in his essay "The Lofty Power of Forests and Streams," about 1090

women were well educated and fairly independent. Li Qingzhao, for example, was born into a prominent scholar-official family and married a high official. She and her husband enjoyed collecting books and art during the years just before the collapse of Song power in northern China. With expansion of the Jin dynasty in the north and the death of her husband, Li returned to her birth family in the lower Yangzi River valley. There she married again to an abusive new husband whom she quickly divorced. During these years, she poured her grief and nostalgia into verse. In 1132, for example, she wrote a poem about her first husband.

> Fifteen years ago, beneath moonlight and flowers,
> I walked with you
> We composed flower-viewing poems together.
> Tonight the moonlight and flowers are just the same
> But how can I ever hold in my arms the same love?

Because of her wealth, status, and talent, Li enjoyed a degree of personal freedom that was an impossible dream for most Chinese women. The renewed emphasis on Confucian morality during the Song dynasty gave men grounds to argue that women should be modest, obedient, and avoid drawing attention to themselves. Women came increasingly under the control of men.

The custom of foot-binding shows how the social status of Chinese women declined during the Song dynasty. Foot-binding probably started during the late Tang period, when professional dancers began wrapping their feet tightly in strips of cloth, perhaps so they could dance on their toes. Then, because people came to think that women with small feet were more beautiful, they started to experiment with wrapping the feet of young girls to keep them small. It worked, and a new social custom was born. By the Southern Song period, some mothers and grandmothers began wrapping their little girls' feet to an extreme degree. Beginning around age five, girls' feet were wrapped so tightly that the arch was broken and the toes were forced to curl under the sole. As a result, some women had very tiny feet; some others had their feet bound less severely. Whether done severely or loosely, the custom of foot-binding in the

Song palace women—the rulers' wives, daughters, or maids—bathe and dress some of the royal children. This 12th-century painting emphasizes the domestic role that women of all social levels were expected to play in Song China.

Song and later times spread steadily down the social ranks, from the wealthy to ordinary commoners and even peasants.

Why did the Chinese decide to bind their girls' feet and why did they do it for so long? People from cultures around the world have done things to permanently modify their bodies, such as tattooing, piercing, or creating decorative scars. Such customs are regarded as normal and desirable by the cultures that practice them, but are often considered strange and deforming by cultures that do not. In China from the Song dynasty up to the beginning of the 20th century, it was generally considered beautiful, refined, and desirable for women to have artificially small feet. Women themselves were proud of their tiny feet; as the 17th-century poet Ye Xiaoluan wrote when she was 16 years old,

> They say lotus flowers bloom as she moves her feet,
> But invisibly, beneath her skirt.
> Her jade toes, tiny and slender,
> Imprint her name wherever she steps.
> Her pure chiffon skirt swirls in a dance.

The custom of binding the feet of young female dancers began at court in the late Tang period and spread down to the common people in the Song period. As men came to think that small feet were beautiful, mothers enforced the practice to ensure their daughters' good marriages. Although women suffered from the custom, they took pride in decorating the small shoes, such as this pair from the late 19th century, which are less than five inches long.

It is also true that women with bound feet could neither walk very far without help nor do much work. They were more likely to remain at home than to go out on their own. Women with bound feet were almost literally put on pedestals, admired for something that partly crippled them. Men and women alike considered foot-binding the mark of an ultracivilized society.

By the early 13th century, China had more people with a high standard of living than had existed anywhere before in the history of the world. But as the various groups of nomadic peoples in the north started to band together, they began to pose a threat that the Song would not survive.

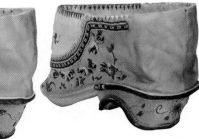

CHAPTER 7

KHANS AND CONQUEST
THE MONGOL EMPIRE

If, on the steppe of Mongolia around 1169, you had been
asked to predict the fate of a nine-year-old boy named
Temujin, his widowed mother, Ho'elun, and his younger
brothers and sisters, you might have imagined two likely
outcomes. They would be captured by members of an enemy
clan and sold into slavery, or as soon as winter set in, they
would die from cold and starvation. In fact, Temujin not only
survived, but he grew up to become the most powerful leader
in the history of the steppes. He went on to conquer a very
large portion of Asia. His childhood name was Temujin, but
history knows him as Genghis Khan.

Around 1100, some 60 years before Temujin was born,
his ancestors had become leaders of a small tribe of horse-
riding people who called themselves Mongols. They were one

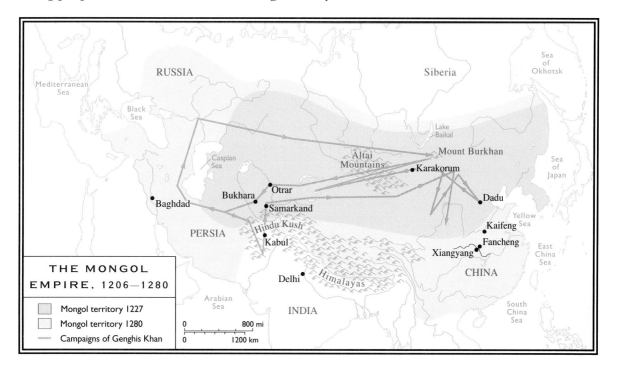

THE MONGOL
EMPIRE, 1206—1280

Mongol territory 1227
Mongol territory 1280
Campaigns of Genghis Khan

0   800 mi

0   1200 km

The people live in black carts and white tents; they breed cattle and hunt, dress in furs and leather, and live upon fermented milk and meat.

—Chinese Daoist priest Qiu Chuji, known as Changchun (Eternal Spring), describing the Mongols in the travel memoir *Journey to the West,* 1220

of several similar groups who lived in the steppe of what is now Mongolia. The Mongols raised horses, lived in round tents made of felt, drank fermented mare's milk, and had religious leaders known as shamans. They believed shamans, while in a trance, had the power to contact gods and spirits of the dead. In the 1140s, Temujin's great-grandfather had led the Mongols into battle against the neighboring Tatars, without much success. The Mongol tribe became small and poor. When he was nine, Temujin's father took him through Tatar territory to be engaged to Borte, the nine-year-old daughter of the chief of a neighboring tribe, the Ongirats. Temujin stayed at Borte's house, as was the custom, while his father returned home. Along the way, his father unwisely accepted hospitality from a group of Tatars and was fed a slow-acting poison. He died several days later.

Temujin's relatives, expecting that the young boy and his family would not survive long after the death of his father, went off to join another clan. Fortunately for Temujin, his mother Ho'elun was a remarkable woman who was fiercely determined to see her family survive. Women of the horse-riding steppe tribes frequently took charge of the herds of horses, cows, sheep, and goats when the men went off to hunt or fight. They could manage a camp, ride horses, and fight with weapons if necessary, and find food, water, shelter when times were difficult. In the words of the *Secret History of the Mongols,* an oral account composed by an unknown author around 1228, "Ho'elun, a woman born with great power, took care of her sons."

When Temujin reached his mid-teens, he took charge of the family. Children of the steppe learned from infancy to ride and take care of animals; boys also learned to wrestle, shoot a bow and arrow, hunt, and fight. Temujin was good at all these things, extremely competitive, ambitious, and a natural leader. His personal qualities soon made him the head of a group of wild and daring teenage boys who became his sworn blood brothers. Gradually, by raiding the herds of neighboring tribes, he built up his family's wealth of sheep, goats, and horses, and with his mother's help he managed the family fortune well. When he felt strong enough to deserve his father-in-law's trust, he went to bring Borte, his wife, back to his own camp. When men from the Merkit tribe kidnapped Borte, Temujin led a raiding party and rescued her. The more successful he was in raiding and in battles against his enemies, the more he gathered followers who accepted his leadership. In the 1180s his supporters assembled at a sacred site in northeastern Mongolia, Mount Burkhan, and pronounced him a khan, or chief. He was given the additional name Genghis (meaning "ocean" or "boundless"). His new title, Genghis Khan, can be translated as Universal Ruler.

IT TAKES A TRIBE

Genghis Khan's rise to world domination was shaped by the nature of tribal society. The word "tribe" is often used loosely, and incorrectly, to refer to any non-Western ethnic group. But the word has a clear and correct meaning that applies particularly to pastoral nomads, people who raise animals in grassland environments. A tribe is a group of people who cooperate as a society. The people of a tribe usually speak the same language, wear similar clothing, and share other things, such as a common ancestor, that tie them together as a group. Members of the tribe often treat one another as relatives, even if they are not actually close blood relatives.

Tribal membership is voluntary. If you don't want to be a member of a tribe anymore, you can leave and try to find another tribe that will accept you. Likewise, tribal leadership

This portrait of Genghis Khan, painted several decades after his death, portrays the great khan as a calm, wise, and somewhat tired-looking man in late middle age. The simplicity of his clothing emphasizes his dignity as the founder of a great empire. He apparently felt no need for fancy ceremonial robes or a royal crown; his accomplishments spoke for themselves.

A 14th-century painting by a Turkish artist shows scenes from daily life in a Mongol military camp, including washing clothes, making a fire, and repairing a saddle. Mounted on their sturdy horses, Mongol men were completely self-sufficient and could travel long distances with very little equipment.

is conditional; a tribal leader is only a leader as long as he can get people to follow him. And tribes make and act on decisions at the lowest possible level. A family will manage its own camp. A clan, or group of closely related families, will manage a grazing territory. Several clans, or perhaps an entire tribe, will cooperate to migrate from one grazing area to another. As in the case of Genghis Khan, the charisma, or natural leadership ability, of a powerful individual might enable him to put together a confederation, or alliance, of several tribes for warfare and conquest. This ability to work successfully at several different levels of organization is an essential characteristic of tribal leader. Genghis Khan would eventually put together the most powerful tribal confederation the world had ever seen.

Genghis first united the various tribes on the steppe into one people called Mongols. His initial aim was to settle old scores and eliminate rival leaders. Feeling little loyalty to his father's faithless relatives who had abandoned him and his family years before, he killed 11 male members of his own clan who were potential rivals. He ruthlessly attacked the Merkits for kidnapping his wife and opposing his rise to power. Soon, in the words of the *Secret History*, the Merkits "ceased to exist as a people." Genghis made a temporary alliance with the Jurchen Jin dynasty of China, and attacked the Tatars, who had murdered his father years before, destroying the entire tribe. He extended his conquests to the west by defeating the Naimans, the last remaining tribe south of the Altai Mountains in what is now western Mongolia.

As he gained military experience, and influenced by the example of China's large permanent army, Genghis began to create a durable military organization. He appointed his most trustworthy friends as bodyguards who took an oath to defend him to the death. He selected trusted followers to be officers of a permanent armed force of almost 100,000 mounted fighters. Troops were organized into units of ten, one hundred, and one thousand men. If any man in a unit tried to run away from the battlefield, the others were responsible for killing him before he could flee; if they failed to do so, all the members of the unit would be executed for desertion. Because Genghis succeeded in battle, his troops were devoted to him and willing to accept the harsh discipline. They went into battle with extra mounts—small but hardy horses whose milk and blood could serve as food for the riders if necessary. The riders were armed with compound bows, which consisted of two arcs, one above and one below the grip, and iron-tipped arrows that they used with deadly accuracy while riding at a full gallop. The Mongol army became a military force of frightening efficiency.

In 1206 the Mongol tribal and clan chiefs met in a Great Assembly at Karakorum on the banks of the Onon River, near Mt. Burkhan, and formally approved his title of Genghis Khan. The assembly also endorsed a campaign to extend Genghis's conquests south of Mongolia. But a military campaign proved unnecessary. When his army confronted the Uighurs and the Onguts, two Turkish-speaking tribes with long experience of governing areas of mixed grasslands, farms, and towns on China's northern frontier, they quickly surrendered.

The Mongol army of Genghis Khan attacks a fortress in Persia as part of his campaign to conquer the Middle East. This illustration is from a 16th-century Indian book on the history of the Mongols. The war elephants in the picture were probably a product of the Indian artist's imagination, because elephants were often used in battle in India. But the Mongols fought with horses, not elephants.

They are never disobedient to orders nor do they ever break their word once it is given. They have preserved the values of earlier ages.

—Chinese Daoist priest Qiu Chuji, known as Changchun (Eternal Spring), describing the Mongols in the travel memoir *Journey to the West*, 1220

Genghis invited Uighur scholars to create a way of writing the Mongol language using the Uighur alphabet. He then instructed his scribes to write down his decrees, or official commands, to serve as laws, not just for the Mongols but "for all peoples who live in felt tents." The decrees dealt with criminal matters, such as murder, and also with administrative law, such as regulations for the military. They also included special rules of steppe etiquette; for example, there were harsh penalties for climbing on the walls of another person's tent, and for polluting scarce drinking water by bathing in a watering hole or running stream.

RESISTANCE IS FUTILE

In 1211, Genghis attacked the Jurchen Jin dynasty in northern China but was unable to defeat it. Enlisting the assistance of the Khitans, whose own Liao dynasty had been defeated by the Jin decades before, Genghis attacked again in 1212. Meeting strong resistance, he besieged, or surrounded, the Jin capital of Zhongdu (site of today's Beijing) from 1213 to 1214. In 1215, the Mongol army finally forced Zhongdu to surrender, and Genghis allowed his troops to loot and destroy the city. This was the Mongols' first conquest of Chinese territory within the Great Wall.

The Mongols' reasons for conquest were complicated. In part they may have been reacting to an environmental crisis on the steppe. During this time, the global climate cooled, and the northern steppe became colder and drier, reducing the quality of the Mongols' pastures. The nomads knew that lands inside the Great Wall could be converted from farmland to pastures to feed their animals. The Mongols also wanted to plunder the riches of a settled society.

For longer than anyone could remember, there had been a steady trade between China and the steppe, with caravans carrying goods in both directions. The nomadic peoples traded leather and minerals to China, and also acted as middlemen for the forest peoples of Siberia who trapped sable, mink, and other furs for trade on the Chinese market. In return, the steppe people especially wanted Chinese silk cloth and metal goods ranging from sewing needles to cooking pots to bronze Buddhist sculptures. The nomads' attitude toward people who lived on farms or in towns was to trade with those who were strong, and raid those who were weak. Many of Genghis's followers were motivated by no larger vision than to capture as much wealth as they could.

Genghis next turned his attention to the west. In 1218 he sent his eldest son Jochi to suppress any remaining opposition among the Naiman, who had surrendered in 1204 but later rebelled against the Mongols. After a successful campaign, Jochi pursued the Naiman refugees south and west across Central Asia. This brought his forces into contact with Khwarazm, a powerful Muslim kingdom northwest of India. Genghis offered to divide the world with the shah, or king, of Khwarazm and to treat him as an honorary son. The shah agreed. But then a local Khwarazmi governor slaughtered a caravan of Mongol ambassadors and traders. In response, Genghis personally led a major expedition against Khwarazm. When the cities of Otrar, Samarkand, and Bukhara refused to surrender, Genghi attacked and conquered them. His forces then selected some children, young women, and craftspeople with useful skills and set them aside as slaves. They slaughtered almost everyone else, whether

A Mongol man's silk robe has "all weather" sleeves, which could be worn long in cold weather or tied behind the robe to allow the wearer to have bare arms in warm weather. Mongol men typically wore such robes over trousers and heavy leather boots.

A Mongol warrior on horseback is equipped with a short, powerful bow, the kind typically used by steppe people in Asia, and a quiver full of arrows. A Mongol warrior's ability to shoot arrows accurately while riding a horse at full gallop made him a dangerous opponent in battle.

or not they had taken an active part in the fighting. When they had finished the killing, the Mongols took everything of value that could be carried away. They were determined to send a message to anyone they threatened to attack: do not resist.

In 1221, Genghis marched southeast to the banks of the Indus River, while his commanders advanced northwest through Persia into Russia. Genghis spent the next year in the Hindu Kush Mountains southeast of Kabul, in today's Afghanistan, resting and learning more about the lands he had conquered. He invited a prominent Daoist priest named Qiu Chuji to travel from China to his camp. As Qiu recalled in a book about his travels, the Mongol leader boasted to him about his humility: "I wear the same clothing and eat the same food as the cowherds and the horse-herders. We make the same sacrifices and we share the same riches. I look upon the nation as a new-born child and I care for my soldiers as if they were my brothers." Qiu replied, "The Chinese people as well as others have acknowledged the emperor's supremacy."

In fact, Genghis was not always good at taking care of his "new-born child." He was never able to establish stable governments in the lands he conquered. It was up to his successors to turn his conquered lands into an empire. In 1227, Genghis died, perhaps from a hunting accident or from illness. At the time of his death, his forces were putting down a rebellion in the Xixia kingdom, in northwestern China. Reported in the *Secret History*, Genghis's last words were chilling: "As long as I can still eat food and say, 'Make everyone who lives in their cities vanish,' kill them all and destroy their homes. As long as I am still alive, keep up the slaughter."

HERE COME THE TAXMEN

In 1229 another Great Assembly confirmed Genghis's selection of his third son, Ogodei, to succeed him. His son Jochi became ruler of the Golden Horde, the Mongol territories of western Asia and southern Russia. Ogodei took the title great khan. He assumed responsibility for the entire Mongol Empire and personally controlled the Mongol homeland and the newly acquired territory of northern China. In 1231 and 1232, Ogodei led forces into southwestern China. They conducted raids there off and on for a decade in an effort to soften up the Southern Song dynasty for invasion. In 1233 and 1234, Ogodei conquered the Jin dynasty and took its capital, Kaifeng, with great loss to life and property.

The Mongols' initial plan was to punish the Jin and their Chinese subjects for their resistance and to turn north China into pastureland to be used by Mongol nomads. A Khitan nobleman named Yelü Chucai persuaded them to follow a more far-sighted policy. Yelü had served the Jin dynasty and then surrendered to Genghis after the fall of the Jin capital of Zhongdu. Appealing to both the Buddhist idea of right action and the Confucian principle of humaneness, Yelü set about convincing the Mongol leaders that they could benefit from ruling China with time-tested Chinese methods. Arguing that taxes bring in more wealth than plunder does, he set up a system for the Mongols to

They are inhuman and beastly, monsters rather than men, thirsting for and drinking blood. . . . They are without human laws, know no comforts, and are more ferocious than lions or bears.

—English historian Matthew Paris describing the Mongols in his book *A History of England*, 13th century

A painting by a Yuan dynasty court artist shows Khubilai Khan and some companions on a hunting expedition. Perhaps as a sign of his identity as both Chinese emperor and Mongol khan, Khubilai wears a Chinese silk gown under a nomad's heavy fur-trimmed coat. The Mongol emperors of China encouraged Mongol men to practice riding, archery, and hunting to maintain their military skills even in times of peace.

exact levies from farmers. Although some Chinese critics felt that Yelü was committing treason by serving "foreign" rulers, he had the satisfaction of helping spare his people from destruction. As he put it, according to the *Record of a Journey to the West,* "is it not a delight... to be in power and have sufficient standing to practice the Way of the Sages [wise men] and sufficient means to confer extensive benefits upon the people?" Historians tend to agree that Yelü was partially successful in his effort to shield the people of north China from the harshest effects of early Mongol rule.

The Great Khan Ogodei and his brothers, and later Ogodei's son and successor, Mongke, continued to pursue Genghis's vision of world conquest, expanding the empire into Russia, Eastern Europe, and the Middle East. In 1253, Mongke sent his brother Khubilai to continue the campaign to take Southern Song China. Khubilai spent most of his career conquering and ruling China, and eventually became better known as the emperor of China than as the great khan of the Mongols. By his time, the Mongol Empire had already begun to split into pieces, each with its own territories and rulers. The brief age of a single, centralized Mongol Empire was already ending.

Ogodei Khan Shows Mercy

RASHID AL-DIN, THE COMPLETE COLLECTION OF HISTORIES, ABOUT 1307

Rashid al-Din, a Jewish convert to Islam, was trained as a doctor but spent most of his career in government, rising to become grand vizier (prime minister) of the Mongol government of Persia. He is best remembered as a historian, whose account of the Mongol Empire is one of the most complete and reliable contemporary sources of information on Genghis Khan and his successors. In this passage, Rashid describes how strict enforcement of the yasa, *the Mongol law code, could sometimes be overruled by mercy.*

According to the *yasa*, it is forbidden for anyone to bathe or wash clothes in running water. One day some Mongol guardsmen saw a Muslim bathing in a stream; they seized him and brought him before the Great Khan Ogodei for sentencing. But the Great Khan felt sorry for the man, condemned by a law of which he was ignorant. Speaking to the Muslim in private, the Great Khan told him to plead that he was a pauper and, having accidentally dropped his last piece of silver into the stream, he waded in to find it. Then the Great Khan secretly sent one of his servants to throw a piece of silver into the stream.

The next morning, the case was heard in court. The Muslim told the story as the Great Khan had instructed him. The Great Khan then sent his guards to the stream to see if they could find evidence that the man was telling the truth. When they returned with the piece of silver, the Great Khan pardoned the Muslim for violating the *yasa*, and sent him away with a reward of ten additional pieces of silver for his trouble.

In this illustration from a 14th-century copy of Rashid al-Din's Complete Collection of Histories, *a Mongol khan and his wife sit outdoors on a portable throne surrounded by their children and servants.*

CHAPTER 8

SULTANS, SLAVES, AND SOUTHERNERS
THE SULTANATE OF DELHI IN INDIA

Qutb-ud-Din Aybak was born a slave but died a king. In the Muslim world, slaves were often battle captives or children of non-Muslims bought or kidnapped from their parents in lands under Muslim control. But slaves were not necessarily confined to low-status work. Because the competition among family members to inherit a throne could be violent, rulers often trusted their slaves more than they did their own relatives. Talented, ambitious slaves sometimes had the opportunity to hold high office, buy their own freedom, and even become rulers themselves. Aybak was a slave-general in the army of Muhammad Ghori, who ruled part of Persia and conquered northern India in 1192. When Muhammad Ghori died in 1202, Aybak took control of his army and had himself named first sultan (king) of Delhi in 1206.

As the first Muslim ruler of Hindu northern India, Aybak immediately introduced Islam into his new realm. His first concern was to get rid of what he regarded as the worshipping of idols. Like some other religions, Islam prohibits making statues or other representations of humans and animals. As a devout Muslim, Aybak was deeply offended by the many religious statues that were displayed in Hindu temples. He ordered the destruction of 27 temples in his capital of Delhi and hundreds elsewhere in north India, using the bricks and stones to construct mosques instead. He closed as many as a thousand temples and built many large mosques all around his kingdom. But, to avoid angering the local population too much, he left some Hindu and Jain temples alone, allowed people to worship as they pleased, and did not make them pay the special tax Muslims normally imposed on non-believers.

Aybak had only about four years to enjoy his status as sultan of Delhi; in 1210 he was killed when his polo pony fell and rolled over on him. (Of Turkish descent, Aybak was a dedicated player of polo, the favorite sport of the Central Asian Turks.) In that brief time he already made big changes that altered the look and sound of northern India. The soaring domes and arches and simple interiors of Middle Eastern-style mosques replaced the high gates, columned halls, and rich sculpture of Hindu temples. Men who converted to Islam or had business with the Muslim government began to wear Muslim-style clothing—baggy trousers, a shirt, and a long jacket—instead of the typical wrapped skirt worn by Hindus. Some women began wearing Muslim-style veils in addition to their brightly-colored wrapped dresses, called saris, and women's clothing in general became more modest under Muslim rule.

Aybak made Persian, already the second language of many people in India and Central Asia, the official language of the sultan's government, reducing the local language, Hindi, to second-class status. To the horror of Hindus, who considered cows to be sacred symbols of the gods' generosity, Muslims in India ate beef. These changes made it clear to many people that Islamic rule in India was there to stay, and many decided they would have to get used to it.

Although the changes Aybak initiated proved lasting, the sultanate of Delhi was not a particularly stable state. It lasted for more than 300 years, but in that time it was ruled by five

This ivory chess piece depicts a mustachioed nobleman, perhaps a king, calmly riding his war elephant into battle. A driver reaches down across the elephant's forehead to attack an enemy horseman who has been seized in the elephant's trunk. An Arabic inscription on the bottom of the piece and the style of the stirrups and saddlecloths indicate that the piece was carved from an elephant's tusk in northwest India in the late 11th or early 12th century.

different dynasties, each overthrowing the other. Overall the sultans of Delhi were a mixed lot, and few of them died natural deaths.

ONE WOMAN WARRIOR AND TWO AMBITIOUS SULTANS

Aybak was succeeded by his son-in-law, Iltumish. When Iltumish died in 1236, he passed the throne to one of his sons, who turned out to be completely incompetent. After just a few weeks, to everyone's shock and amazement, Aybak's daughter, Raziya, seized the throne and proclaimed herself sultan. Her bold move succeeded, at least for a short time. As her contemporary the Indian historian Minhaju-s Siraj recalled in his *Stories of the Reign of Nasir*, "Sultan Raziya was a great monarch. She was wise, just, and generous, a benefactor to her kingdom... and the leader of its armies." Her success and her downfall came from acting like a man.

As sultan, Raziya dressed in typical Muslim men's clothing, wore a sword, and refused to wear a veil or cover her hair as Muslim women normally did. At first people seemed to accept her authority as they would that of a male sultan, and she even forced the ruler of Bengal to surrender to her. According to Siraj, she then made a political mistake. She became romantically involved with an Ethiopian slave named Yakut, and soon appointed him to be her main adviser. This was too much for traditional Muslim men who were already upset by what they saw as Raziya's unfeminine behavior. Public opinion turned against her. Raziya and Yakut fled from Delhi to the Panjab region in northwest India. Their political enemies captured them, and executed Yakut immediately.

Raziya managed to charm, and then marry, one of her captors, and in 1240 the two of them launched an attack on Delhi to recover her throne. Raziya, letting a man take charge for once, allowed her husband to plan the crucial battle. They lost, disastrously, and were murdered by peasants as they fled from the battlefield. As Minhaju-s Siraj wrote shortly after Raziya's death, "She was endowed with

The sultan Ala-ud-din Khalji constructed the Alai Darwaza building in Delhi next to the highest Islamic tower in the world. The building's arches and domes are characteristic of Islamic architecture, and its use of red sandstone and white marble provide a striking contrast.

all the qualities befitting a king, but she was not born of the right sex, and so in the estimation of men all these virtues were worthless. (May God have mercy on her!)" According to another, less sympathetic, historian, she should have stayed at her spinning-wheel, making "cotton her companion and grief her wine-cup." In other words, women had no role to play in public affairs. That opinion apparently was widely shared, and there were no more female sultans in Muslim India.

A little more than 50 years after Raziya's death, in 1296, Ala-ud-din Khalji became sultan by murdering his uncle, a ruler honored for his wisdom and moderate policies. Ala-ud-din then rid himself of potential rivals by immediately executing all his friends who had helped him kill the former sultan. Then he set about expanding the area under Delhi's control.

As sultan, he was almost constantly at war, and nearly doubled the sultanate's territory. Along the way he picked up a slave, a Hindu convert to Islam named Kafur Malik, who became his constant companion. Kafur was an even more enthusiastic conqueror than his master, and he became known as a ruthless destroyer and looter of Hindu temples. A youthful eyewitness to these events, the Muslim historian Zia ud-Din Barani, recorded in his *History of the Reign of Shah Feroz* that Kafur returned from one campaign with booty that included 20,000 horses, 612 elephants, 241 tons of gold and countless boxes of jewels and pearls.

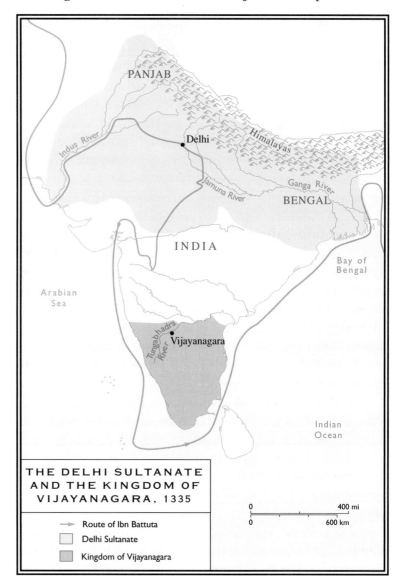

THE DELHI SULTANATE
AND THE KINGDOM OF
VIJAYANAGARA, 1335

0   400 mi
0   600 km

→ Route of Ibn Battuta
    Delhi Sultanate
    Kingdom of Vijayanagara

Despite his engagement in bloodshed and plunder, Ala-ud-din was a conscientious ruler. He made serious efforts to build the country's economy, especially by encouraging farming and increasing the production of textiles. For centuries, India had been the world's leading producer of cotton cloth. In the 12th century, the spinning wheel, which had long been used by the Central Asian Turks, was introduced into India. Spinning wheels replaced the old method of hand-spinning and improved the quality of cotton thread as well as the speed with which it could be produced. Around the same time, craft workers developed new ways of printing patterns on textiles cheaply and rapidly. Using these technological improvements, India became the world's most important source of colorful cotton textiles, which were exported in large quantities to Southeast Asia. According to Barani, Ala-ud-din's greatest achievement was not his conquests but the "cheapness of grain, clothes, and the necessaries of life.... This was the wonder of the age, and something that no other monarch was able to achieve."

Tughluq, who took the throne in 1316, was another former slave. Like many sultans, Tughluq had family problems. He died when a building collapsed on him, an event that some people suspected was arranged by his son. That son, Muhammad bin Tughluq, then inherited the throne. Muhammad bin Tughluq was a complex person. He was intelligent and well educated, and could read Islamic texts in Arabic, write elegant verse in Persian, and discuss classical Greek philosophy. He is also remembered as "the bloody sultan" for his habit of ordering officials who displeased him to be whipped to death. He was fairly moderate in his religious beliefs and had friendly discussions with Hindus and Jains, but he harshly punished any Muslims whom he suspected of having improper beliefs.

The sultan's wealth attracted many foreign Muslim artists, writers, military men, and specialists in other fields, who came to Delhi hoping to work for him. One of the visitors was the Moroccan world traveler, Abu 'Abdallah ibn Battuta, who arrived in Delhi in 1333. In his account of his travels, Ibn Battuta described Delhi as "vast and magnificent...the

I shall be compassionate to you and give you such favors that your fellow-countrymen will hear of it and come to join you.

—Sultan Muhammad bin Tughluq to his guest Ibn Battuta,
The Travels of Ibn Battuta, 1347

largest of the cities of Islam in the East." Recalling his first meeting with Muhammad bin Tughluq, he described him as "the Master of the World, a tall, robust, white-skinned man seated, his legs tucked beneath him, on a gold-plated throne." The sultan took his hand, held it, and said in Persian: "This is a blessing; your arrival is blessed; be at ease." Off to a good start, Ibn Battuta gave the sultan the impression that he was an expert in Islamic law. The sultan immediately appointed him to be a judge in Delhi. Although Ibn Battuta did not speak Persian well and apparently handled few legal cases while he was a judge, the sultan relied on him for advice, and he grew quite wealthy. After a few years the sultan appointed him to be his ambassador to China. This was exactly what Ibn Battuta, the greatest traveler of the medieval world, wanted, and he left India to continue on his travels.

THE NORTH ATTACKS, THE SOUTH RESISTS

While northern India was firmly in the hands of Muslim rulers, a Hindu kingdom defiantly held out in the south. In 1336, two brothers, Harihara and Bukka Sangama, rebelled against the sultanate of Delhi and led a series of campaigns to stop the expansion of Muslim power in south-central India. They founded Vijayanagara, Land of Victory, and built a new capital city, also called Vijayanagara, on the banks of the Tungabhadra River, near the southern edge of India's central plateau. Located in a natural fortress of tall granite cliffs, the city seemed to say to its northern neighbors, "here is a line you dare not cross." Over the next two centuries, local Hindus built dozens of major Hindu temples in and

A Generous and Scary Sultan

ABU 'ABDALLAH IBN BATTUTA, TRAVELS, 1347

Abu 'Abdallah Ibn Battuta, born in Morocco in 1307, traveled to more places in the world than anyone else of his time. He spent several years at the court of Muhammad bin Tughluq, sultan of Delhi, where he served as a judge, was treated kindly by the sultan, and lived in great luxury. His writings clearly show that he was always a little frightened of the sultan, whose actions were hard to predict. Depending on his mood, the sultan might give a person a purse full of gold one day and order the same person tortured to death the next day. In this passage from his account of the Sultanate of Delhi, Ibn Battuta describes the sultan's character.

When Sultan Tughluq died his son Muhammad became master of the realm without any rival or opponent. . . . Of all the people this king loves most to give presents and also to shed blood. His door is never free from a poor person who is to be enriched and a living person who is to be killed. Stories of his generosity and bravery as well as of his cruelty and severity towards offenders are repeated widely among the people. Despite this, he is the humblest of men and the most devoted to the administration of justice and to the pursuit of truth. The sayings and principles of Islam are preserved by him. He lays great stress on the performance of prayer, and those [Muslims] who neglect to pray are punished by him. He is one of those kings whose good luck is unique and whose happy good fortune is extraordinary; but his dominating quality is his generosity.

This illustration from an Arabic book of travelers' tales shows a "Prince of the Eastern Islands" with two Arab astrologers. Ibn Batutta was one of many Arabs who served as advisers to South Asian rulers in the era of the sultanate of Delhi.

The Lotus Mahal temple, built in the state of Vijayanagara in the 15th century, combined Islamic-style arches, domes, and vaults with South Indian–style towers, birds, and human riders on rearing animals. It, therefore, reflected the region's mixed culture during the time.

In the perfection of his great wisdom, God has decreed that there be a just and competent ruler of mankind so that…the rules for managing the affairs of mankind might be kept and preserved on the right path.

—Indian Islamic writer
Shaikh Hamadani,
The Treasuries of Kings,
late 14th century

around the city, and devout Hindus from all over the subcontinent made pilgrimages to the capital.

Vijayanagara soon controlled almost all of southern India. The kingdom grew wealthy from farming and trade, and from the offerings that pilgrims gave to the temples. Traders from India's southern ports sailed to Southeast Asia and brought back information about new developments in the wider world. In the early 15th century, Vijayanagara assembled an army of mercenaries, or soldiers-for-hire, including Hindus, Muslims, and Christians from all around the Indian Ocean. It also hired military technicians who knew how to make gunpowder and brass cannons. Vijayanagara thus held off its neighbors and enjoyed peace and security for another century and a half.

The sultanate of Delhi was seriously challenged at the end of the 14th century by the invasions of Timur Leng (Timur the Lame, known in Europe as Tamerlane), a Turkish Muslim who claimed to be a descendent of Genghis Khan and whose leg had been permanently damaged in battle. In 1398 Timur crossed the Jamuna River and attacked Delhi. When Delhi fell, on Timur's orders his soldiers slaughtered the city's Hindu population but spared the lives of its Muslims.

They stripped the city of its wealth, and his officers carted huge amounts of gold and silver back to Timur's capital, Samarkand. Timur hoped to use the treasure he took from India to fund an invasion of China, but he died before that plan could be carried out. In a memoir written near the end of his life, he explained the destruction of Delhi: "Although I wished to spare them, I could not succeed, for it was the will of God that this calamity should befall the city." Will of God or not, the Delhi sultanate lost control of much of its former territory, and never fully recovered.

In the weakened Delhi sultanate of the 15th century, Hindus and Muslims made good progress toward understanding one another better. Some Hindus converted to Islam; many others began to wear Muslim-style clothing, enjoy Muslim music, and appreciate the Islamic ideals of justice and good government. Hindus and Muslims started to marry one another. Many Muslims developed a more relaxed attitude about "idols."

The process of reconciliation was helped greatly by the work of a humble, illiterate poet named Kabir. The son of a poor family of weavers, Kabir was born sometime around 1440; no one outside his family paid much attention to the event. As a young man he showed both an unusual gift for language and a deep insight into spirituality. Though his family background seems to have been Muslim, he was influenced by the Hindu concept of *bhakti*, an all-embracing personal love of God. When he grew up, he became an outspoken critic of all forms of organized religion; he began writing poetry in which he insisted that true religion

In this Persian miniature, Timur Leng, who traced his ancestry to the Mongol leader Genghis Khan, leads a hunt for a lion, demonstrating his personal courage and concern for keeping his troops fit. Known to the West as Timur the Lame (or Tamerlane), he established a large empire in Central Asia and northern India, but died before he could realize his plan to conquer China.

At the Vitthala temple in the southern Indian state of Vijayanagara is a shrine to Garuda, the divine eagle ridden by the god Vishnu. The temple chariot's wheels were cut from separate blocks of stone so that they could rotate on their axles. The faithful used a similar vehicle made of wood to carry dancing girls to the temple during festivals.

lies only in the heart, not in buildings or rules or sacred books. Many of his contemporaries, Hindu and Muslim alike, thought of Kabir as a saint, and they flocked to listen to him recite his poems. Kabir himself never learned to write, but hundreds of his verses were written down by his followers and collected into books. He repeated his message in poem after poem:

> As the seed contains the oil,
> And the fire's within the flint,
> So the Divine sits in the temple of yourself;
> Realize it if you can.

In the turbulent world of the Delhi sultanate, Kabir's poetry was an enduring message of reconciliation.

CHAPTER 9

KHAN AND EMPEROR
THE YUAN DYNASTY IN CHINA

When 21-year-old Marco Polo arrived in China in 1275 with his father, Maffeo, and his uncle, Nicolo, they had been traveling for three years, all the way from Venice, Italy. They had made their way along the Silk Road, with many stops for business and rest. Nicolo and Maffeo were old hands at travel in China, for they had already been to Khubilai Khan's court in 1265, and were impressed enough with China and with its Mongol rulers to return. Marco, making his first trip, was dazzled. From the moment he arrived, he felt sure that he was in the biggest, richest, and best-governed state in the world. As he explained in *Travels,* written in 1298, he was amazed to see at the great khan's summer capital "a huge palace of marble and other ornamental stones" with "fully sixteen miles of parkland well watered with springs and streams." He thought that Europe had nothing to compare with that.

In an illustration for a 15th-century French edition of Marco Polo's book Travels, *Khubilai Khan gives Polo a golden pass that will allow him to travel freely anywhere in the empire. The artist who created this image accepted as truth Polo's claim that he was a high official in the Mongol Empire with direct access to Khubilai Khan—a claim doubted by many people in his own time, as well as by many scholars today.*

The Polos were in no hurry to leave; they stayed in China for 17 years. According to his book *Travels,* Marco was lucky enough to get a job with Khubilai's government, and while it is not at all clear what his responsibilities were, his work did seem to involve a lot of travel around the empire. He may have been a sort of roving inspector, looking at local conditions in different places and then reporting back to the central government. If Marco Polo had made his trip to China at a time when it was ruled by almost any other dynasty, he would never have been offered an official

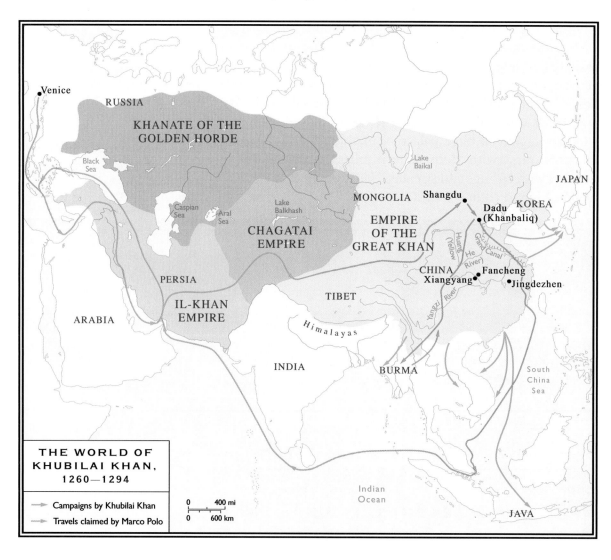

THE WORLD OF KHUBILAI KHAN, 1260—1294

→ Campaigns by Khubilai Khan

→ Travels claimed by Marco Polo

0   400 mi

0   600 km

position. He was able to work for the government only because Khubilai Khan, the founder of the Yuan dynasty, was its head.

We have only Marco Polo's own word that he went to China and served in the government there. In his book, *The Travels,* he clearly exaggerated his own importance, and there is no other evidence that he was ever an important official in the Mongol government of China. Some people in his own time called his account "the book of a million lies," and some modern scholars believe that Marco never even went to China, but simply recorded the stories of other travelers, including his father and uncle. Whether Marco was an eyewitness or not, his descriptions are generally accurate, and it is certainly true that Khubilai Khan employed foreigners as officials.

Khubilai was elected great khan of the Mongols at a Great Assembly held in northern China in 1260, but he did not devote much of his energy to the Mongol Empire. By then the empire was divided into four basically independent parts, and Khubilai concentrated on being emperor of China. Khubilai consulted with Liu Bingzhong, a Chinese scholar recognized for his knowledge of the Three Teachings (Confucianism, Daoism, and Buddhism), about the name for his new Mongol dynasty of China. Liu suggested calling the dynasty Yuan, meaning "origin" or "primary." Khubilai liked the idea that his dynasty would mark a return to an ancient pattern of good government, and he adopted the name.

A Chinese civilian administrator, perhaps a tax collector or the magistrate of a rural county, rides with a Mongol bodyguard. The painting is set in wintertime; the civilian wears a Chinese-style cloth hood and cape, while the Mongol, armed with bow and arrows, wears a heavy fur coat.

BACK TO A SIMPLER LIFE

Northern China, which had been ruled by the Jurchen Jin dynasty since 1126, was already securely in Mongol hands by the time Khubilai came to power. In the 1250s Khubilai designed and built two new capital cities for his Chinese empire. One city, in the mountains north of present-day

Paper money was invented in China during the Song dynasty and used extensively during the Mongol Yuan dynasty as well as in Korea. European visitors to China were amazed that printed paper, with no value of its own, could be used to buy and sell goods. After about 1500, the Ming dynasty mostly abandoned the use of paper money and relied instead on silver coins.

Beijing, was called Shangdu ("upper capital"), and was used during the hot summer months. The other, used during the rest of the year, was called Dadu ("great capital") or Khanbaliq ("khan's city"), built near the site of today's Beijing. Khubilai's adviser Liu Bingzhong designed the imperial palace, a walled enclosure stretching half a mile from east to west and three-quarters of a mile from north to south. The compound contained hundreds of buildings, from grand halls, temples, and offices to residences for the emperor, his principal wife, and his many concubines.

Liu Bingzhong worked with Guo Shoujing, the foremost Chinese mathematician, astronomer, and engineer of his time, to plan and build a system of canals to supply water for the capital. Guo also designed a 135-mile-long extension of the Grand Canal to bring rice and other goods from the south up to the new capital at Dadu. This canal caused great hardship to the workers who built it, but it greatly improved the transportation network of northern China. The Arab traveler Rashid al-Din remarked in his *History of the World* that the canal made it possible "to bring to the capital the vessels of all the provinces in Cathay." (Cathay was an old European name for China.)

Khubilai then focused his resources on a campaign to defeat the Southern Song dynasty and secure his control over all China. In 1268 the Mongol commander in charge of the campaign encountered heavy resistance from the fortified towns of Xiangyang and Fancheng on the Han River, a major tributary of the Yangzi, in central China. The general wrote to Khubilai, "The forces I am leading consist entirely of Mongol cavalry; encountering barriers of mountains and rivers, stockades and forts, without Chinese forces I can do nothing." Khubilai ordered a Chinese general who was fighting on the Mongol side to create an inland navy to attack the towns. The navy, borrowing a Song tactic, used catapults to hurl explosive bombs from the ships into the cities. Both cities fell in 1273.

The next year Khubilai appointed a Mongol nobleman to conduct the final campaign against the Southern Song. The commander assembled an immense force of 200,000 infantry, cavalry, and sailors and moved slowly down the Yangzi, winning over some Song forces and defeating others. If a town resisted, the Mongols captured it and then massacred the whole population. With that example in mind, the Southern Song capital of Lin'an surrendered without a fight in February 1276. The last Song emperor and his court were taken north, where Khubilai and his wife Chabi treated them well. But some Song loyalists fought on, rallying around an infant heir to the throne. Three years later, facing certain defeat in a naval battle, a Southern Song official lifted the child onto his back and jumped into the sea, committing suicide to avoid capture. Khubilai's control of China was complete at last.

Khubilai had some very strong opinions about how China should be governed. He did not trust the scholar-official class, suspecting (correctly) that many well-educated Chinese looked down on the Mongols. He also wanted to satisfy the Mongols who wished to hold positions of power. So he got rid of the examination system and gave many important posts to non-Chinese, to strengthen Mongol control of the state. Khubilai then divided the whole population of China into four groups on the basis of ethnic and geographical background. On top were the Mongol warriors, the backbone of the empire's military forces. They controlled the Bureau of Military Affairs, which operated in secrecy and became the top decision-making body for the whole government. Next came people of Central and West Asian heritage, including Turks, Muslims of various backgrounds, Tibetans, Persians, and even a few Europeans. The Polos were part of this group. Many of these people were appointed to government departments that controlled taxation, trade, and finances. These departments were completely separate from the old Chinese bureaucracy.

An artist who refused to serve in the government of the Yuan dynasty painted this young Chinese nobleman on horseback. By dressing the young man in a clothing style from many centuries earlier and having him hold an old-fashioned long bow rather than the short compound bow of the Mongols, the artist presents a subtle protest against Mongol rule in China.

The third social group was made up of all "people of Han," meaning the peoples of northern China—including Khitan, Jurchen, and even Koreans. They had borne the brunt of the wars and hardships of the mid-13th century. Now, in the Yuan period, they were required to provide more than their fair share in taxes, labor, and military service. In the 1280s, for example, some 3 million Han laborers were forced to build the northern extension of the Grand Canal.

The fourth group into which Khubilai divided China's population was the Nanren (southerners), who were among the last to surrender to the Yuan. The Yuan administration excluded them from all civil and military positions and generally banned them from carrying weapons, although some exceptions were made. But the Mongols tended to ignore the southerners, who were basically left alone to benefit from the more peaceful and prosperous economy of southern China. Excluded from official positions and paying relatively low taxes, many southerners put their energy into commerce. A number of market towns and manufacturing towns, such as the porcelain-producing center at Jingdezhen

A Chinese farmer uses a water buffalo to plow a flooded rice paddy; the stubble of the previous harvest of rice plants is visible in the foreground. This painting suggests that for most Chinese peasants in the countryside, life went on as usual under Mongol rule.

in the southern province of Jiangxi, reached new heights of prosperity during the Yuan period. Trade from southern ports to the South China Sea and the Indian Ocean continued to thrive.

Initially, Khubilai Khan's government reforms worked as intended and placed the Mongols firmly in power. But they created two problems for the future. First, many members of the scholar-official class were angry that there were no more civil service exams, which greatly reduced their prospects for official careers. They deeply resented the foreigners, some of whom could not even speak Chinese well, who had been appointed to government positions. Second, many common people were extremely unhappy about the high taxes and all the labor they were expected to do. In general, China under the Mongols felt like an occupied country, and many people were looking forward to a time when the foreigners could be driven out again.

Meanwhile, scholars unable to hold office devoted themselves to pastimes such as art. Paintings of bamboo became especially popular. The common people attended performances of Chinese opera to distract them from their troubles. Many of the operas written during this period featured stories from China's glorious history, before anyone had ever heard of Mongols.

Although Khubilai Khan treated China like a conquered land, and supported policies to separate people by their backgrounds, he was very broad-minded on the subject of religion. Marco Polo reported that Khubilai told one foreign visitor, "There are four prophets who are worshipped and to whom everybody does reverence. The Christians say their God was Jesus Christ; the Saracens [Muslims] Muhammed; the Jews, Moses; and the Buddhists, Gautama Sakyamuni... and I do honour and reverence to all four." Khubilai indi-

Khubilai Khan's army attacks a Chinese city on the Yangzi River in this scene from a history of the Mongols written in Persian and illustrated by an Indian artist in the 16th century. The artist has imagined a scene of war elephants attacking an Indian-style walled city. The Mongols did not use war elephants in China, but they used horses, firearms, catapults, and other weapons to attack cities, and they gave their enemies a simple choice: surrender or die.

cated that he considered all these prophets to be just different faces of one god "who is greatest in heaven, and more true, and him I pray to help me." The great khan was happy to rule an empire that included Buddhists, Daoists, Muslims, Jews, Christians, and others, and to allow all of them to worship their own gods in their own fashion.

KHUBILAI BITES OFF MORE THAN HE CAN CHEW

In 1259, after decades of warfare, Khubilai signed a peace treaty with the king of Korea, who acknowledged Khubilai as his superior. In each of the next 35 years the Korean court sent diplomats to Dadu bearing tribute—even including, when the Korean king learned that Khubilai suffered from gout (a disease that causes painful swelling of the joints), fish-skin shoes designed to ease the pain in the great khan's feet. Khubilai married his daughter to the Korean crown prince and was very protective of Korean interests. He also attempted to control the entire Korean peninsula more closely than any previous Chinese state had done, and he made heavy demands on the Koreans to support his policies toward Japan.

In 1268, Khubilai sent a mission to establish contact with Japan, but the Japanese ruler was offended by being described in a letter from the great khan to the emperor of Japan as the "king of a small state" and sent the mission back with no reply. Three more Yuan missions over the next five years were also unsuccessful, and Khubilai was worried about Japanese contact with the Southern Song. In 1274, he dispatched 30,000 troops in a fleet of nearly 700 ships to force Japan to recognize the Yuan. They won some early battles on the coast of Japan but then were driven away by a storm, with a loss of 13,000 men.

After three more Yuan ambassadors were killed by the Japanese, in 1279 Khubilai began to assemble a fleet of thousands of ships and 125,000 soldiers and sailors, which sailed for Japan in 1281. The Japanese held out behind a newly constructed wall until another storm hit and the Yuan troops were again forced to retreat with great losses.

The priest has to teach religion, and the king to guarantee a rule which enables everybody to live in peace.... The heads of the religion and of the state are equal, though with different functions.

—Tibetan Buddhist lama (monk) Phagspa in a report to Khubilai Khan, late 13th century

This scene from a 14th-century scroll painting called The Fascination of Nature *shows animals and insects preying on each other in an "eat-or-be-eaten" struggle for survival. The artist painted this scene as a way of dramatizing the difficult moral choice Chinese scholars experienced during the Yuan dynasty: should they work for the Mongols and live as prosperous officials, or avoid working for the conquerors at the risk of poverty?*

After planning and then canceling a third invasion, Khubilai gave up on the idea of establishing relations with Japan, let alone trying to conquer it.

Khubilai had little more success gaining respect in Southeast Asia. In 1273 he sent three representatives to Burma to get that country to recognize his authority. The Burmese king, who boasted on a pagoda he built that he was "the master of 3,000 concubines...the commander of thirty-six million soldiers," and the "swallower of 300 dishes of curry daily" promptly executed the representatives. Khubilai then spent more than ten years trying to force Burma into submission. His army succeeded in destroying the Burmese capital at Bagan, but not in conquering the country. A Yuan effort to invade the island of Java, in present-day Indonesia, in 1292 was defeated when a Javanese prince first welcomed the Mongols and then attacked their army by surprise. By the time Khubilai died in 1294, his unsuccessful expeditions of conquest had put a serious strain on China's military and financial resources.

After Khubilai died, nine more emperors occupied the throne of the Yuan dynasty. Chengzong, Khubilai's immediate successor, controlled military expenses by canceling plans for further conquest and by making peace with the Turks of Central Asia. Renzong, the fourth Yuan emperor, tried to appease the Chinese scholar-official class by bringing back the examination system in 1313. He also made a good impression by appointing Zhao Mengfu, a descendant

The Mongol Pony Express

" MARCO POLO, TRAVELS, 1298

In his account of China during the reign of Khubilai Khan, Marco Polo seemed deeply impressed by how effective the emperor's government was. His book Travels *contains a lengthy description (condensed here) of the system of roads and fast riders that could take a message from one part of the vast empire to another in a matter of days. He was all the more impressed because Europe had nothing to match such a fast and efficient communications system.*

From the city of Khanbaliq [Dadu, now Beijing] there are many roads leading to the different provinces, and upon each of these...at the distance of twenty-five or thirty miles...here are stations...called *yamb* or post-houses. At each station four hundred good horses are kept in constant readiness, in order that all messengers going and coming on the business of the grand khan...may have relays, and, leaving their tired horses, be supplied with fresh ones....The royal messengers go and return through every province and kingdom of the empire with the greatest convenience and ease, in which the grand khan exhibits a superiority over every other emperor, king, or human being....

When it is necessary that the messengers should proceed with extraordinary speed as in the cases of giving information of a disturbance in any part of the country, the rebellion of a chief, or other important matters, they ride two hundred, or sometimes two hundred and fifty miles in the course of a day. On such occasions they carry with them a tablet having on it a picture of a falcon, as a signal of the urgency of their business..., and they wrap their bodies tightly [with cloth bandages, for support], bind a cloth around their heads, and push their horses to the greatest speed.... Changing in the same manner at every stage, until the day closes, they perform a journey of two hundred and fifty milesthey continue thus until they come to the next post-house at twenty-five miles distance, where they find...other horses fresh and in a state to work; they spring upon them without taking any rest, and continue.... Messengers qualified to undergo this extraordinary degree of fatigue are held in high estimation.

Thieves get to be officials and officials behave like thieves,

The good can't be told from the bad, alas, how sad!

—Anti-government song popular during
the late Yuan dynasty, about 1350

of the Song royal family, head of the Hanlin Academy, which was the top imperial academy for Confucian learning. Zhao, the best painter and calligrapher of his time, had begun his official career under Khubilai. Some Chinese scholars criticized Zhao for working for the Mongols, but others admired him for always doing his work with integrity. For a time it seemed that the Yuan dynasty would succeed in winning the support of the Chinese people after all.

The emperors who followed Renzong were undistinguished. The Mongols kept themselves segregated from the Chinese, discouraged intermarriage, and monopolized the highest government jobs. They were widely resented, and Han Chinese who served the Yuan government were often regarded as selling out to an alien dynasty. By the 1350s, the dynasty was near collapse due to bad administration, famine, and popular unrest. Looking for some sort of salvation in a time of trouble, many people turned to the White Lotus sect of Buddhism, which predicted that at any moment Maitreya, the Buddha of the Future, would appear. Those who believed in the teachings of the White Lotus sect would be spared; those who doubted would be destroyed. This faith inspired many rebellions that soon drove the Mongols from the central plain of China.

This travel pass was issued to a Mongol official during the Yuan dynasty, giving him the authority to travel freely throughout China. In his book Travels, *Marco Polo claimed that he had been given such a pass, made of gold, by Khubilai Khan himself.*

CHAPTER 10

WARRIORS RULE

KAMAKURA AND ASHIKAGA JAPAN

A samurai nobleman in ordinary civilian dress acts as a judge in a legal case. Under Japanese military rule, nobles called daimyo, *or great names, performed all government functions in the territories that they controlled. They owed obedience and loyalty only to the shogun.*

By the time he died in 1181, Taira Kiyomori considered himself master of all Japan. During the first half of the 12th century the imperial government in Heian-kyo had grown weak under the Fujiwara family's system of child-emperors and regents. Powerful military clans in the provinces arose to take advantage of this weakness in the capital; clan leaders surrounded themselves with armed men called samurai ("those who serve"), who were sworn to loyalty or death. Tensions had steadily grown between two of the most powerful clans, the Taira and the Minamoto. In 1156 and again in 1160 the two clans fought; Taira Kiyomori's army finally crushed the Minamoto clan and executed their leaders.

As the head of the most powerful clan, Kiyomori moved his headquarters from the western provinces to Heian-kyō, married his daughter to the heir to the throne, and settled down to take over the old Fujiwara system of controlling the imperial government. In 1180 he had the pleasure of seeing his infant grandson take the throne as Emperor Antoku. Kiyomori expected that his heirs would dominate Japanese politics for generations to come.

Japan had changed far more than Kiyomori realized, however. While Kiyomori was transforming himself into a pleasure-loving Heian nobleman, the surviving Minamoto were sharpening their swords at their eastern base in Kamakura. In 1185 the Minamoto, led by the young brothers

Yoritomo and Yoshitsune, struck back. Taking the young emperor with them, the Taira fled westward with the Minamoto in hot pursuit. The end came with a great naval battle on April 24, 1185, at Dan-no-Ura in the western Inland Sea. The Taira forces were wiped out. When the noblewoman who had been taking care of the seven-year-old emperor saw that the situation was hopeless, she picked him up and said, "I will not fall into the hands of the enemy. I shall accompany our Sovereign Lord [the emperor]. Let those of you who will, follow me." She jumped overboard, drowning with the boy in her arms. Japan was now in Minamoto hands.

In an act of self-destructive jealousy, Minamoto Yoritomo refused to give his brother and best general, Yoshitsune, credit for the naval victory over the Taira. The brothers quarreled, and Yoshitsune was forced to flee for his life. To avoid capture and to dramatize his selflessness and lack of bad intentions toward his brother, Yoshitsune committed ritual suicide by disemboweling himself (cutting out his own intestines) with his sword. This was the first notable instance of a form of suicide that became common among defeated military men in succeeding centuries. After his death, Yoshitsune was celebrated as a hero for his nobility and loyalty.

Yoritomo, on the other hand, is remembered as the morally flawed but politically successful founder of a new type of Japanese government. In 1192 Yoritomo formally adopted a new title, *Sei-i tai-shogun* ("great general who suppresses outlanders"). Usually shortened to shogun, or general, this was the hereditary title of Japan's real ruler for almost the next seven centuries. Yoritomo left the emperor on the throne but assumed all authority himself as the head of a military government. Avoiding Taira Kiyomori's mistake, he refused to

A wooden statue of Minamoto Yoritomo, founder and first shogun of the Kamakura shogunate, portrays him in court dress with baggy trousers, a wide over-jacket, and a tall hat. This statue was kept in a Shinto shrine at Kamakura, an indication that after his death Yoritomo had been elevated to the status of a god.

move to the capital, which was now simply called Kyoto, meaning "capital city." Instead he fortified his clan's base at the small town of Kamakura, which gave its name to the period when the Minamoto shoguns were in power. At Kamakura he established a *bakufu,* or tent government, implying that he was permanently on a military campaign to defend the emperor. He gained allies by making the leaders of other powerful clans daimyo ("great names"), governors of large military estates. The daimyo were supported by stewards who managed their estates, and by their private armies of samurai.

Yoritomo died in 1199, and his sons inherited his title, but proved to be weak successors. Twenty years later, his widow's family, the Hojo clan, seized power by establishing a regency for the Minamoto shoguns. Just as the Fujiwara and Minamoto families had taken over the power of the

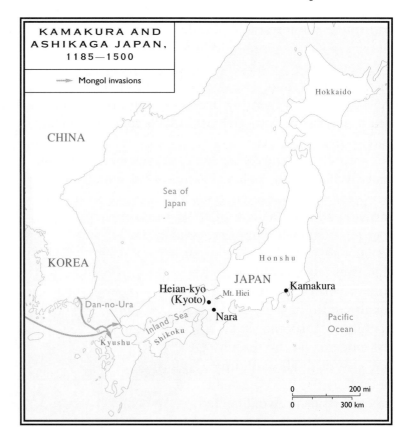

This painting shows a battle between the samurai armies of the Taira and Minamoto clans in 1159. At the time, the imperial government in Heian-kyo was weak, and the Taira and Minamoto were fighting a civil war in which the winner would gain supreme power in Japan. The war ended in victory for the Taira clan, but they remained in power for only 25 years.

emperors without becoming emperors themselves, so the Hojo family now exercised all the power of the shoguns without becoming shoguns themselves. During the Kamakura period, while military politicians competed for power, new kinds of Buddhism competed for the hearts and minds of the people.

BE TRUE TO YOUR SCHOOL

The dominant school of Buddhism in the Heian period had been Tendai, named after a holy mountain in China. In Japan, its headquarters was at Mount Hiei, northeast of the capital Heian-kyō. Tendai focused on the Lotus Sutra, a Buddhist scripture that stressed salvation through strict discipline and meditation. Also influential was the Shingon or True Word school, which emphasized the transmission of secret teachings from master to disciple.

During the 12th century, a new school, called Pure Land, became popular. The Pure Land school taught that you did not need to be male, study texts, or become a monk

A senior priest of the Shingon sect of Buddhism holds a vajra, or diamond thunderbolt, symbol of indestructible truth. Shingon was one of several Buddhist sects that originated in China and became powerful and influential in Japan. It emphasized sacred rituals performed by priests and monks who had been initiated into their secrets.

to be saved. All you had to do was take a vow of devotion to Amitabha, the Buddha of Infinite Light; call on his name; and you would be reborn in the Western Paradise, a beautiful, rich, and peaceful land filled with gods and humans, all of whom got their every wish. The Pure Land master Shinran argued that evildoers might be even more acceptable to Amitabha Buddha than good people, because evildoers had to rely completely on Amitabha's mercy and could not hope to attain salvation on their own. As recorded in his student's "Collection Inspired by Concern of Heresy," "if even a good man can be reborn in the Pure Land, how much more the wicked man!" Shinran believed that monks should be able to marry and he did so himself. Shinran was exiled from the capital because of his ideas and his lifestyle. His school, however, persisted in a less radical form.

In the 13th century, a Buddhist teacher named Nichiren created yet another school of Buddhism. The son of a humble fisherman, Nichiren studied at the Tendai temple on Mount Hiei. He devoted himself completely to the Lotus Sutra, and preached that only through its teachings could people attain salvation. He attacked the Tendai, Shingon, and Pure Land schools as inadequate, and criticized the Hojo family for supporting those schools. With his typical sharpness, he was recorded by a follower as saying: "The world is full of men who degrade the Lotus of Truth, and such [men] rule this country now." In 1260 Nichiren predicted that the Mongols would soon invade to punish Japan's rulers for their errors.

When the Mongols attacked Japan in 1274, Nichiren gained a large following. More and more outspoken in his criticism of the government, Nichiren was arrested, charged with insulting the Hojo regents, and exiled to a small island in the Sea of Japan. From there he wrote, in a letter to a follower: "Birds cry but shed no tears: Nichiren does not cry, but his tears are never dry." In other words, he refused to cry out in sorrow, but he was always sad to be cut off from his followers. Nichiren called on his followers to respond to the persecution of their sect by trying even harder to spread his message. His disciples became militant missionaries, and the Nichiren sect exists in Japan to this day.

Late in the Kamakura period another type of Buddhism, Zen, became very influential because it appealed to the military aristocrats, among others. Zen emphasized the discipline of meditation; in fact the word *zen* (in Sanskrit *dhyana* and in Chinese *chan*) means "meditation." Zen originated in sixth-century China among Buddhist monks who were influenced by Daoist ideas of spiritual development. Zen masters taught that enlightenment comes from within, not from scriptures or rituals. Zen students were urged to free themselves from the limitations of logic and reason by meditating on puzzles that have no answer, such as the typically Zen question, "What is the sound of one hand clapping?" Zen students were also required to learn self-discipline, for example, by sitting motionless for long periods of time, in order to rid their minds of worldly distractions.

The purpose of Zen meditation and self-discipline was to prepare the mind for enlightenment, a sudden, nonverbal flash of understanding of the truth behind surface realities. This approach appealed to samurai, who often studied in Zen temples. They used Zen methods to strengthen their warrior skills and their ability to endure suffering. From Kamakura times on the discipline and concentration of Zen became closely associated with the code of Bushido, the Way of the Warrior.

This samurai helmet and suit of armor is made of painted leather and metal plates held together by silk cord. Like European knights, Japanese samurai engaged in hand-to-hand combat with one another in wartime, and they wore elaborate armor to protect themselves against swords and steel-tipped arrows.

For over thirty years I had tormented myself by putting up with all the things of this unhappy world. . . . In my fiftieth year, then, I became a priest and turned my back on the world.

—Former aristocrat Kamo no Chomei, *An Account of My Hut*, 1212

Real Simple

YOSHIDA KENKO, ESSAYS IN IDLENESS, ABOUT 1350

The shift in political power away from the emperor toward the samurai military government in the Kamakura and Ashikaga periods made many people think about the proper way to live. Was it worthwhile to try to have an official career, or was it better to withdraw into private life? For many members of both the samurai class and the old court aristocracy, the simplicity and discipline of Zen Buddhism was the answer. It became fairly common for samurai, at some point in their careers, to turn their backs on the world and become monks. Yoshida Kenko was a celebrated poet and court official who became a Buddhist monk in 1324. In a short book called Essays in Idleness, *Yoshida talks about his preference for living simply but in comfort. His essay on adopting a Zen lifestyle gives a cheerful view of "leaving the world of dust" to live in seclusion.*

There is a charm about a neat and proper dwelling house, although this world, 'tis true, is but a temporary abode. Even the moonlight, when it strikes into the house where a good man lives in peaceful ease, seem to gain in friendly brilliancy.

The man is to be envied who lives in a house, not of the modern, garish [tacky] kind, but set among venerable trees, with a garden where plants grow wild and yet seem to have been disposed with care, verandas and fences tastefully arranged, and all its furnishings simple but antique.

A house which multitudes of workmen have devoted all their ingenuity to decorate, where rare and strange things from home and abroad are set out in array, and where even the trees and shrubs are trained unnaturally—such is an unpleasant sight, depressing to look at, to say nothing of spending one's days therein. Nor, gazing on it, can one but reflect how easily it might vanish in a moment of time.

The appearance of a house is in some sort an index to the character of its occupant.

FOR WHOM THE WIND BLOWS

When the Mongols invaded Japan in 1274 and 1281 they were defeated by the forces of the Kamakura shogunate, assisted by storms that came to be called kamikaze, meaning "divine winds." But it was not clear whose prayers produced the winds—-maybe Nichiren's, maybe someone else's. Others gave credit to Hachiman, the Shinto god of war, or to the ancestor of the emperor, the Shinto goddess Amaterasu. Whoever was responsible for the victories, they produced a crisis for the Hojo regents.

Up until the Mongol attacks, wars in Japan had been civil wars. One side would win, one side would lose. The winning leader would seize the property of the losers and give it to his supporters. This time the Mongols were defeated and either died or sailed away; there was no booty to divide up. Many daimyo and samurai had also fought bravely, and some had died. They, or their families, expected a reward. The Hojo regents gave away some of their own property to their loyal supporters, but it was not enough. The samurai began to feel very dissatisfied with the regency.

In 1333, an unusually energetic and intelligent emperor, Godaigo, tried to recover the imperial throne's lost political authority. The Hojo regency, feeling threatened, sent a military commander, Ashikaga Takauji, to force Godaigo to give up the throne. But Takauji was not happy with the Hojo regents, and found Godaigo's appeal for loyalty to the throne attractive. So, he switched sides and used his army to occupy Kyoto in defense of the emperor. After a three-year-long complicated struggle for power, Takauji changed his mind again. He finally proclaimed himself shogun and

The law [of Buddhism] is the Truth inherent in all its perfection in every living creature.

—Zen Buddhist master Muso Soseki, sermon at the opening of Tenryu monastery, 1345

When there is nowhere
That you have determined
To call your own,
Then no matter where
* you go*
You are always going home.

—Poem by Zen Buddhist
master Muso Soseki,
about 1345

set up his own tent government in Kyoto. Godaigo was forced into exile in the mountains south of Nara.

In 1335 the influential Zen master Muso Soseki advised Godaigo to send an official mission to re-establish friendly relations with China—for the first time in 500 years. The mission to China was a success, but Godaigo's larger aim of restoring imperial authority was frustrated by Japan's military leaders. Takauji's successors, the Ashikaga shoguns, also followed Muso's advice and cultivated good relations with China. When they wrote to the emperor of China they deliberately disguised their roles as shoguns, referring to themselves as "kings" and addressing the Chinese emperor as Son of Heaven. They did not mention the emperor of Japan at all.

The renewed relationship with China was profitable for both countries, and was especially important to the Ashikaga shoguns because their estates did not provide enough money to pay the expenses of the military government. Both Japan and China valued the relationship and benefited from it. Japan exported fans, scrolls, and fine swords to China and imported silk, porcelain, books, paintings, and copper coins from China.

ZEN ARTS

The trade between the two countries made it easier for Japanese and Chinese Zen temples to be in contact. Japanese monks who studied in China were impressed by the discipline of Chinese Zen masters, who could sit in meditation for hours. As the Japanese master Dogen recalled in a conversation with his disciple Ejo in the 1240s, "When I was staying in the Zen lodge in Tiantong [China], the venerable Jing used to stay up sitting [in meditation] until the small hours of the morning and then after only a little rest would rise early to start sitting again." Over the centuries, Zen monks in China had also explored how exercising restraint and patience in the arts could help lead to enlightenment. These Zen ideas profoundly influenced Japanese art.

Japanese Zen temples, for example, were typically made of unpainted wood and other natural materials in a plain, simple style. Soon even the rich and powerful began to build their houses in this understated style, instead of in the fancier form of Heian palaces. Zen temples, and the buildings inspired by them, often had gardens that were designed with a "small is beautiful" attitude. Some Zen gardeners created gardens using only oddly shaped stones and carefully raked gravel. Raising bonsai, miniatures trees carefully tended in shallow ceramic pots, was a Zen-inspired pastime that took a lifetime of patience.

Tea had been known in Japan during the Heian period, but was not very important to Heian society. In the early 13th century the Japanese Zen master Yeisei Myoan brought tea seeds back from China and planted a tea garden next to his temple in Kyoto. Myoan called tea the secret of long life, and promoted the idea of serving tea to guests. Within two centuries the Japanese developed the tea ceremony, one of the most characteristic expressions of Japanese Zen Buddhism. The host of the tea ceremony carefully prepares

A classic Zen garden at the Daitokuji Temple in Kyoto uses raked sand, rocks, moss, and a few small plants to create an imaginary landscape. Reflecting the simplicity and discipline of Zen Buddhism, Zen art often follows the principle that "less is more."

fine tea in simple but elegant ceramic bowls, and serves the drink in a small room free from distractions, enjoying the total experience of tea, simplicity, and beauty with a small group of friends.

Painting and swordsmanship were Zen arts that had much in common. Zen painting emphasized speed and spontaneity, and artists created their paintings in black ink with just a few fast, confident strokes of the brush. Swordsmen practiced their art until they could strike a deadly blow more quickly than the eye could see, or the mind could think. Zen painting and swordsmanship looked effortless when done by a master, but neither could be done well without years of focused, disciplined practice.

Zen ideals also influenced a new type of drama, Noh ("ability"), that became very popular with the samurai class.

A male performer of Noh drama portrays a princess by wearing a female mask, a gold crown, and an elaborately embroidered silk kimono appropriate to a female character. Noh drama, slow, stylized, and filled with dramatic tension, was popular with Japan's samurai warrior class.

Actors performed the plays, which often featured supernatural themes, on a nearly bare stage, wearing masks and elaborate silk robes. They acted almost in slow motion, with very stylized music and dance. The aim of the actor's technique was to build a powerful sense of dramatic tension, so that the smallest gesture, such as the curl of a finger or a tilt of the head, could seem filled with significance. Zeami, the most prominent author of Noh plays, believed that the most important quality of Noh was *yugen*, or mysteriousness, and he wrote in an essay called *The Attainment of Yugen* that it was "the mark of supreme attainment in all the arts and accomplishments."

In the warrior society that dominated Japan after the Heian period, women had lower status than before. The worlds of the samurai fortress and the Zen temple were masculine worlds in which women had no role. The scattered domains of the daimyo aristocracy were much less hospitable to women of talent than the imperial court had been. Women dominated Heian literature, but few women writers are known from the Kamakura and Ashikaga periods. The era of Lady Murasaki and *The Tale of Genji* was over.

The Ashikaga shoguns are remembered as enthusiastic supporters of Zen arts, but not as capable rulers. In 1467 another civil war, called the Onin War, broke out. It lasted a decade and destroyed much of Kyoto. After the end of the Onin War, real authority in Japan lay in the hands of the daimyo, who controlled their domains from castles that combined the elegance of palaces with the strength of fortresses. They no longer had any loyalty to the shoguns and were simply regional warlords who fought constantly with one another. This time in Japanese history was so filled with armed conflict that it came to be known as the Warring States period. The decline of the Ashikaga shogunate was so complete, that when the dynasty ended in 1573 hardly anyone noticed.

One cannot be sure
of living
Even until the evening.
In the dim dawn light
I watch the waves of the wake
Of a departing boat.

—Poem by the Buddhist priest Shinkei at the time of the Onin Wars, about 1470

CHAPTER 11

FRESH DAWN
KORYO AND EARLY CHOSON KOREA

In 1388, General Yi Songgye faced a difficult decision. His master, the king of Korea, had ordered him to attack China, which he did not want to do. The Korean kingdom of Koryo had given its loyalty to the Mongol rulers of China more than a century before, and the king had not fully accepted the idea that China's new Ming dynasty had defeated his Mongol allies. Also the king was angry that Ming troops occupied a small corner of the Korean peninsula. So the king sent General Yi to attack China. But General Yi was well aware that the Ming dynasty was securely in power in China, and that the Mongol dynasty had been overthrown.

Yi was a practical man from a humble background. He had been a military man all his life, and had fought successfully against Japanese pirates on Korea's coast and Chinese rebels who raided the Korean frontier. He knew that his army could never win if it invaded China. So he led his army to the bank of the Yalu River—the border with China—but he did not cross. Instead he turned back,

This portable Buddhist shrine, made of bronze, silver, and wood and plated with gold, is a miniature version of a Korean Buddhist temple. Its interior shows an image of the Buddha with Bodhisattvas (Buddhist saints) and disciples, while guardian figures on the doors keep evil away.

seized the Korean capital, and, four years later, overthrew the king and proclaimed himself the founder of a new dynasty. His new state, which he called Choson ("fresh dawn," an ancient Chinese name for Korea), endured for more than 500 years.

The kingdom of Koryo that General Yi overthrew had been in power since 936. Its founder, Wang Kon, built his state in the mid-10th century on a foundation of Chinese ideas and institutions that he adapted to what he thought would work in Korea. As one historian recorded in the *History of the Koryo Dynasty,* compiled in 1451 from earlier records, King Wang Kon reminded one of his advisers that Korea was "far removed from China," and he saw no reason to "strain...unreasonably to copy the Chinese way." Still, just as the Japanese had followed the plan of the Chinese Tang dynasty capital Chang'an to design their capitals at Nara and Heian-kyo, King Wang Kon built his new capital, Kaesong, on the same plan. And, he organized his government mostly following the Chinese model.

Even though King Wang Kon used the Chinese system of civil service exams to appoint officials on the basis of their abilities, Korea remained a highly aristocratic society. The Wangs shared power and status with bone-rank families, many of whom could trace their ancestry back to the sixth century, when King Kim Wonjong of Silla had invented bone ranks. Just as in Heian Japan at the same time, certain families became powerful by supplying the Koryo kings with wives. The Kims married three daughters to a king in the early 11th century and then dominated four kings during the first half of that century. Four sons of the Yi family became high officials and married their daughters into the royal line. Later the Ch'oe family controlled the throne for several decades on the basis of their own military power. They established their own palace guard of 3,000 men and an army of slave soldiers.

During this time, the government of Koryo had to deal with the Mongol Empire that was rising in the west. In 1231, when the Koreans killed a Mongol ambassador, the Mongols launched a full-scale invasion of Koryo. The

Koryo general responsible for the northwestern frontier region mounted a strong defense at the town of Kuju. The Mongols surrounded the town for a month without being able to take it. Finally, the Koryo government made a deal with the Mongols and ordered Kuju to surrender. A senior Mongol commander visited the town and exclaimed, as recorded in the *History of the Koryo Dynasty,* "Since my youth I have followed the army, and I am accustomed to seeing the cities of the world fought over and defended, but I have never seen anyone attacked like this and refusing to surrender to the end." For the next two decades, the Mongols attacked Koryo over and over.

The Ch'oe were unable to defend Korea from the Mongols but they also refused to make peace with the invaders. In 1258, some civil officials who were concerned that the Mongol invasions would destroy the country joined with some generals and assassinated the Ch'oe leader. The following year the Wang prince who was next in line for the throne, Wonjong, surrendered to the Mongols, who then supported his claim to the throne against his rivals. By 1273, the Koreans had stopped resisting the Mongols.

For the next century, the Wang royal line ruled Korea in close cooperation with their Mongol overlords. King Wonjong and his descendants married Yuan dynasty princesses, took Mongol names, wore their long hair in the Mongol fashion, and used the Mongol language. Real authority in Korea after 1280 was in the hands of the Mongol-run Eastern Expedition Field Headquarters, which served as a military government for the lands northeast of China. Peace with the Mongols benefited Koryo as Korean traders began to export porcelain and books to China and Mongolia in return for such things as cotton from India and gunpowder from China. The large number of Koreans returning from visits to China and elsewhere in the Mongol Empire with new ideas and information enriched Korea intellectually. When uprisings against Yuan rule began in China in the mid-14th century, the Koryo kings remained among the Mongols' most loyal allies.

MAKING FRIENDS WITH THE MING

When General Yi Songgye came to the throne in 1392 as founder of the new Choson dynasty, Korea was ready for some big changes. King T'aejo, as General Yi was eventually called, carried out a sweeping program of reform based on the principles of Confucian government. One important measure was land reform, by which estates of the old Koryo elite were broken up and redistributed. Some of the land, of course, went to General Yi's chief supporters. As one Confucian adviser remarked in his essay "On Land" around 1400, "Although the distribution of land to the people may not have reached the standard set by the ancient sages [wise men], the new land law has restored equity and balance."

In good Korean style, many Koreans attributed General Yi's success to his ancestors. In fact, Yi owed his position not to his family but to his military skill and the support of

KINGDOM OF CHOSON
IN THE REIGN
OF KING SEJONG,
1419—1450

0   100 mi
0   150 km

CHINA

Yalu River

Sea of
Japan

Kaesong

Hanyang
(Seoul)

Yellow
Sea

KOREA

JAPAN

Confucian scholars. According to the official court history, the *Veritable Records of King T'aejo*, he claimed that he had accepted the throne only because "people's wishes are such that heaven's will is clearly manifested in them; and no one should refuse the wishes of the people, for that would be to act contrary to the will of heaven." Like his contemporary, the founder of the Ming dynasty in China, Choson T'aejo of Korea clearly thought of himself as the people's choice.

The Choson founder and his successors established close relations with the Ming dynasty that ruled China at the same time and adopted much of its system. In a symbolic gesture acknowledging the authority of the powerful Ming rulers, they adopted the Ming calendar. Choson ambassadors visited the Ming capital at least once a year. T'aejo used the Chinese examination system and, unlike the rulers who came before him, tried to make sure it provided men of talent to help run the state. With a similar concern for the people, T'aejo and his advisers decided to move the capital from landlocked Kaesong to Hanyang (today's Seoul) on the

Wooden printing blocks carved in Korea in the mid-13th century to produce a complete set of Buddhist scriptures in Chinese are now kept in a remote mountain temple in South Korea. The 81,258 blocks contain a total of more than 52 million words and were used to print 6,568 volumes of Buddhist sacred books.

practical grounds that it was centrally located, near a seaport, and a convenient place for the people.

King T'aejong, T'aejo's successor, strongly encouraged the creation of a Korean publishing industry instead of relying on China, which he thought was too far away to be the only source of books. In 1403, according to a contemporary scholar's essay "On Printing," the king remarked to his court: "If the country is to be governed well, it is essential that books be read widely." He also wanted to develop a new way of printing. One crack or scratch could spoil a whole wood printing-block, so he declared, "It is my desire to cast copper type [make metal pieces for each individual character] so that we can print as many books as possible and have them made available widely." Although moveable metal type had already been used in China, the Chinese still printed most of their books with woodblocks. In 1403 the Koreans built the first really successful moveable metal-type printing machine—50 years before the German printer Johannes Gutenberg (who usually gets all the credit) made his moveable type press. Moveable type turned out to be very good for the simplified Korean script that was soon to be invented.

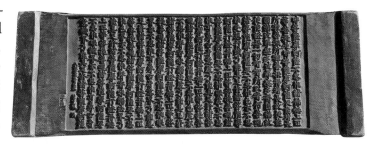

Book printing in East Asia was usually done by the woodblock process rather than by using moveable type. Each wooden block was carved on both sides with Chinese characters that could be lightly coated with ink and printed onto a piece of paper. This block is part of the set that was used to print a complete edition of Buddhist scriptures in mid-13th century Korea.

A GREAT KING AND HIS GRAND INVENTIONS

When T'aejong died in 1419, the 22-year-old crown prince took the throne. Known as King Sejong, he became one of the most accomplished and enlightened monarchs to be found anywhere in world history. As a boy he quickly learned the Chinese classics, and he was interested in knowledge of all kinds. As king, he created an extensive system of education. In 1420, he established the Hall of Worthies, a kind of research institute that produced some remarkable inventions. Placing less emphasis on Buddhism

continues on page 144

Why Should We Toil and Suffer?

HISTORY OF THE KORYO DYNASTY, COMPILED IN 1451

In Koryo's social structure, farmers placed second after scholars, but in fact, most of them lived very hard lives. In addition to working the land and paying taxes, they had to provide unpaid labor on public projects. Slaves ranked even lower and suffered more, whether they were owned by the state or by private families. Descendants of slaves could not hold office for eight generations, and efforts to free the slaves were defeated on the grounds that the freed slaves might cause trouble. In the 1170s, however, military men who felt insulted by aristocrats killed the king, opening the way to popular revolt. For the next two decades, there were many popular uprisings against the government and the aristocrats. Farmers, slaves, and others were active in the revolts. Even after the military restored order in 1196, slaves continued to dream of liberty and conspire in rebellion as the following account makes clear.

In King Sinjong's first year [1198], the private slave Manjok and six others, while collecting firewood on a northern mountain, gathered public and private slaves and plotted, saying, "Since the coup [seizure of power] in the year [1170] and the countercoup in the year [1173], the country has witnessed many high officials rising from slave status. How could these generals and ministers be different from us in origin? If one has an opportunity, anybody can make it. Why should we still toil and suffer under the whip?"

The slaves all agreed with this. They cut several thousand pieces of yellow paper and wrote the character *chong* [adult man] on each one as their symbol. They pledged: "We will start from the hallways of Hungguk Monastery and go to the polo grounds. Once all are assembled and start to beat drums and yell, the eunuchs [neutered male palace servents] in the palace will certainly respond. The public slaves will take control of the palace by force, and we will stage an uprising inside the capital, first killing Ch'oe Ch'unghon [the general who had suppressed rebellions in 1196] and others. If each slave will kill his master and burn the slave registers, there will be no people of humble status in the country, and we can all become nobles, generals, and ministers."

On the date set to meet, their numbers did not exceed several hundred, so they feared they would not succeed and changed their plans, promising to meet at Poje Temple this time. All were ordered: "If the affair is not kept secret, then we will not succeed. Be careful not to reveal it." Sunjong, the slave of Doctor of Legal Studies Han Ch'ungyu, reported this incident to his master. Ch'ungyu told Ch'oe Ch'unghon, who seized Manjok and more than one hundred others and threw them into the river. Ch'ungyu was promoted to warder [watchman] in the Royal Archives, and Sunjong was granted eighty *yang* [one *yang* = 1.325 ounces] of white gold and freed and upgraded to commoner status. Since the remaining gang members could not all be executed, the king decreed that the matter be dropped.

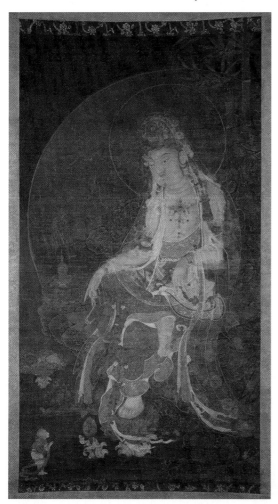

This painting of Avelokitesvara, the Bodhisattva (Buddhist saint) of Infinite Mercy, dates from the Koryo dynasty. Many Koreans, including workers and slaves, believed that the mercy of Buddhist saints would allow them to be reborn in the Western Paradise, thus escaping from the misery of this world.

continued from page 141

than the Koryo kings had done, Sejong founded an advanced academy for Confucian studies called the Hall for Illustrating the Cardinal Principles. In an essay praising the hall, a scholar at the time said the students "study, deliberate, counsel, and assist one another to reach full understanding of the relationships between ruler and minister, father and son, husband and wife, elder brother and younger brother, friend and friend."

Partly through the influence of King Sejong's schools, Koreans in the Choson era developed a rather conservative type of Confucianism, like that of Song and early Ming China. Choson Confucians tended to value men over women. They encouraged domestic rituals that showed respect for the ancestors and could be conducted only by men, and they opposed the practice, once common in Koryo Korea and Heian Japan, of husbands moving into the households of their wives' families. In an essay titled "On Remedying the Wedding Rite," one Confucian scholar warned King Sejong: "The man who enters the woman's house thereby confuses the meaning of husband and wife." Choson Confucians also tried to discourage widows from remarrying.

In an effort to improve his subjects' morals, King Sejong decided to publish a book filled with stories about people who set good examples. According to a scholar's "Preface to Illustrated Conduct of the Three Bonds," in 1431 the king instructed officials to identify loyal, respectful, and pure people and "have their pictures drawn and their stories compiled and distributed inside and outside the capital so that all the ignorant

Buddhist priests during the Koryo dynasty used this ceramic jar to sprinkle holy water on participants in religious ceremonies. It combines the beauty and high technical quality of Korean ceramics with the specific requirements of an object made for Buddhist ritual use.

husbands and wives, by looking at them with sympathy, may be easily stimulated to proper behavior."

Up until Sejong's time, all books in Korea were either written in Chinese or used Chinese characters to write Korean phonetically. Many Korean scholars had no problem with using Chinese to write their books. In the *Veritable Record of King Sejong,* one scholar was recorded as saying: "Only such peoples as the Mongolians, Tanguts, Jurchens, Japanese, and Tibetans have their own writings. . . . this is a matter that involves barbarians and it is unworthy of our concern." King Sejong, however, thought education in Korea was suffering because it was so awkward to write Korean using Chinese characters.

In 1443 he appointed a committee of scholars to create a new Korean script. After trying it out himself, he approved it. In an essay entitled "Correct Sounds to Instruct the People," he explained its advantages: "The sounds of our language differ from those of Chinese and are not easily communicated by using Chinese graphs [characters]. Many among the ignorant, therefore, . . . have been unable to communicate. Considering this situation with compassion, I have newly devised twenty-eight letters. I wish only that the people will learn them easily and use them conveniently in their daily life." Koreans quickly adopted the script and it is used to this day. Most scholars think it is the simplest and most rational writing system in the world.

The scholars at the Hall of Worthies, where the script was invented, made other contributions to Korean culture. Agricultural specialists studied Chinese and Korean farm manuals and interviewed experienced farmers to write a book called *Straight Talk on Farming,* published in 1429. Four years later medical scholars produced a manual that explained almost 1,000 diagnoses and more than 10,000 cures. It included 1,500 different techniques of acupuncture, the science of inserting needles at certain points on the body to release natural chemicals that block pain.

In the 1430s Korean scientists made a set of new bronze instruments for King Sejong's royal observatory that allowed his astronomers to observe the movements of the planets and other heavenly bodies with unprecedented accuracy. Eight years later, technicians announced the invention of a rain gauge, a tool that helped predict the size of the crops that would be harvested. The observatory also included an elaborate water clock. It used a regulated flow of water into a bronze container to float a wooden rod, which, at precise time intervals, released iron balls from a rack. The energy of the balls rolling down ramps powered devices that beat a drum, struck a bell, and caused puppets to pop up in a window holding signs telling the correct time. One of King Sejong's court historians wrote in his record of Sejong's court, "No one seeing it does not heave a sigh and aver [swear] that we Koreans certainly had nothing like this in former times."

King Sejong's clock was based on an earlier model that had belonged to Khubilai Khan, which a Korean ambassador to the Mongol court had described in detail. The Chinese builders of Khubilai Khan's clock had taken the basic design for the iron-ball mechanism from a book in Arabic published in Damascus, Syria, in 1206. This clock is an example of the continuing travel of ideas and inventions along the Silk Road.

Korea's King Sejong commanded that this bowl-shaped sundial, along with others like it, be set up in the capital so that ordinary people could easily know the time. Made to a high standard of precision, these sundials can tell the time within a range of a few minutes.

The mind is a moonlit autumn field,
Ripe with the gold fruit of knowledge.

—Buddhist master Kyunyo, *Eleven Devotional Poems,* about 970

In 1450 Sejong died of cancer at age 52 and was succeeded by his eldest son, King Munjong. Munjong ruled for only three years, but people remember him for his interest in history. From the kingdom's beginning, Choson historians had followed the Chinese practice of recording daily events at court in texts called the *Veritable Records.* Munjong's scholars used these and other records to put together a *History of Korea.* Their book was modeled on the official histories that Chinese scholars had written about every major dynasty since Han times. It included events at court, genealogies, tables, essays, and biographies. In the book's dedication, one scholar described history as a model: "It is said that when one makes a new ax handle, one examines an old one as a model, and that when one builds a new carriage, one uses an old carriage as a model. This is so we can learn lessons from the past."

Its talented early rulers built a firm foundation for the kingdom of Choson that made it strong enough to overcome many difficulties in later times. General Yi's family retained control of the throne, the country remained united, the culture was passed from generation to generation, reforms were proposed, and the upper class expanded to include increasing numbers of families from the countryside. Despite tensions, Choson lasted until 1910, one of the most accomplished, peaceful, and durable dynasties in human history.

CHAPTER 12

RISE AND SHINE
RULERS AND TREASURE SHIPS IN MING CHINA

Zhu Yuanzhang was born in 1328 into a poor farm family in central China. As a young boy he listened to his grandfather tell stories about the last days of the Song dynasty before the Mongol conquest some 50 years earlier. He briefly attended a local elementary school where he learned to read at a basic level. When he was 16, his father, mother, and elder brother were struck down by the plague, the deadly disease known as the Black Death that spread throughout Eurasia. He and his younger brother buried the dead. Many years later, he placed a tombstone over their grave and wrote an inscription for it in which, with evident anguish, he recalled: "Buried without inner or outer coffins, the bodies wrapped in worn old garments, placed in a scant

The Ming state encouraged farmers to grow grain and vegetables, but they also urged them to sell what they did not consume. The state established peace and order and provided copper and silver currency that allowed the development of numerous towns and cities, filled with shops and marketplaces, that were among the most prosperous in the world.

three-foot grave, what ceremonial offerings could we make?" The orphans went to stay in a local monastery; when food there ran out, Zhu became a beggar. After several years, he returned to the monastery where he may have gained a little more education.

In the troubled mid-14th century, as the Yuan dynasty weakened, the White Lotus sect of Buddhism—which preached that the world would soon end with the coming of Maitreya, the Buddha of the Future—gained many followers. Fearing that the monastery where Zhu was living was a base for White Lotus rebels, Yuan troops attacked and destroyed it. With no way out, Zhu joined a local group of White Lotus rebels, which already included some of his boyhood friends. He married the rebel chief's adopted daughter and attracted his own followers within the rebel group. Zhu was tall and strong, with a dark complexion, a prominent forehead and chin, large nose, big ears, and bushy eyebrows. People who met him were struck by his unusual looks and thought he must have some special destiny. Disgusted by power struggles within the rebel group, Zhu gathered together his own followers and headed south.

For the next 10 years Zhu led his army into battle after battle in central China, fighting against both Mongol troops and rival rebel leaders. He developed relations with Confucian scholars who had turned against the Yuan regime, but he also kept in touch with his old White Lotus friends, who understood the anger and frustration of the common people. In 1363 Zhu's forces defeated an important rival in a major naval battle on Boyang Lake, in south-central China. He then moved against another competitor in Suzhou, a wealthy city in the lower Yangzi River valley. Zhu besieged Suzhou in 1367 and took it in 1368. That victory gave him the confidence to proclaim himself the founder and first emperor of a new dynasty, which he called Ming, meaning "brilliance." The name Ming could be understood in two ways. To some people, it would seem like a reference to Confucian enlightened government, while to others it would recall the brilliance of the Maitreya Buddha worshipped by the White Lotus rebels.

TAIZU TAKES COMMAND

In 1368 Zhu launched a great offensive against Yuan strongholds in northern China. On September 9 of that year, as Zhu's forces approached the capital city of Dadu, the last Mongol ruler of China fled north into the steppe. Zhu took Dadu with little bloodshed, though his armies looted and largely destroyed the Yuan imperial palaces. He established his own capital at Yingtian (today's Nanjing) on the Yangzi River.

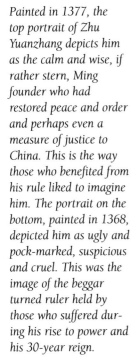

Painted in 1377, the top portrait of Zhu Yuanzhang depicts him as the calm and wise, if rather stern, Ming founder who had restored peace and order and perhaps even a measure of justice to China. This is the way those who benefited from his rule liked to imagine him. The portrait on the bottom, painted in 1368, depicted him as ugly and pock-marked, suspicious and cruel. This was the image of the beggar turned ruler held by those who suffered during his rise to power and his 30-year reign.

The founder of the Ming dynasty, known to history as Taizu ("grand ancestor"), remembered his own humble origins and tried to serve the interests of the common people. He established public schools at the province and county levels, and urged local scholars to set up community schools in the villages. He restored the civil service examinations that had been of little importance during the Yuan and made them the main way of recruiting officials. He wanted to ensure that good students from whatever background would be able to succeed in the examinations and become officials. When students from wealthy and powerful families in the lower Yangzi valley took a large share of the degrees in 1373, he suspended the examinations. According to a history compiled in the 17th century, he complained: "We sincerely sought worthies but the world responded with flunkies." He later restored the examinations, but made sure that students all over the realm would have equal opportunities to succeed in them.

Ming Taizu wanted scholars and officials to serve the interests of the

This well-dressed young woman of the 15th century is embroidering a piece of silk fabric, enhancing its value before it is sent to the court as tribute or tax or sold in China or abroad. The Chinese admired embroidery as an art form, and it continued to earn women money and respect during the Ming.

common people. In 1392, he asked two teachers about conditions, such as rice prices in the countryside, where they worked. When they could not answer his questions, he charged them with not understanding worldly matters and with being ignorant of conditions among the people. Remarking that such teachers would ruin even good students, he exiled them both to remote posts on the frontier.

Following the suggestion of his Confucian advisers, Ming Taizu reformed the country's laws. He approved measures to protect debtors and small merchants from unscrupulous moneylenders and other people who engaged in unfair business practices. The laws also contained special protections for women, even though on the whole the status of women declined under Ming rule. To show that his new laws applied to everyone, he prosecuted many of his early supporters and high officials for engaging in corruption.

Ming Taizu had a less admirable side. He allowed officials to torture suspected criminals when they were being questioned, and he applied harsh punishments, such as slow death by slicing, for crimes such as treason. In some cases, he not only executed people accused of crimes, but wiped out their entire families. As he got older, and especially after the death of his wife, he seemed to become more suspicious of his officials and advisers. In 1396 he executed an imperial censor for being too critical. This was shocking to Confucian officials, because it was the censor's job to criticize the emperor when he felt it was necessary, and he was supposed to be immune from retaliation.

Ming Taizu's approach to the world was largely defensive. According to the *Veritable Records of Ming Taizu,* he gave a speech to his officials on October 30, 1371, in which he pointed to the fate of the Sui dynasty and cited the ancient saying that "the expansion of territory is not the way to enduring peace, and the over-burdening of the people is a cause of unrest." He added that the Ming should punish foreign states beyond its frontiers that threatened it, but should not take up arms against those that posed no danger. Toward the end of his reign, he listed 15 states, including Korea, Japan, Annam, and Java, that the Ming should never invade.

When Ming Taizu died in 1398, some scholar-officials and commoners must have been relieved, but others may well have been sad. Life, after all, had greatly improved for the vast majority of Chinese since the founding of the Ming, 30 years before. With the death of Taizu's eldest son and heir, there was a struggle for power. At first Taizu's 21-year-old grandson took the throne. Soon Taizu's fourth son, Zhu Di, whose mother may have been a Korean secondary wife of Taizu's, announced that he was his father's true choice to inherit the throne, and that the young emperor had no right to it. Zhu Di and his nephew fought a brutal civil war to determine who would be Taizu's successor; Zhu Di won the war in 1402.

Zhu Di, who is usually known by his reign name Yongle (meaning "perpetual happiness"), followed his father's example and ruled with both persuasion and force. He was a good judge of character and chose well qualified men as his top officials. He made the scholar-official class happy by putting together a massive collection of all the Chinese literature that had ever been written. But he also relied too heavily on eunuchs (men who were castrated in childhood) as his personal staff within the imperial palace, and put them in charge of a force of secret police that operated outside of the law.

Since ancient times, Chinese emperors, like rulers in many other early states, had employed eunuchs as personal servants. Eunuchs could work in the family quarters of the palace without the emperor worrying that they might become involved with the imperial wives and concubines. Because they had no families of their own, eunuchs were expected to devote themselves entirely to the emperor they served.

In China, emperors were often tempted to give too much power and responsibility to eunuchs, who could be used to impose the rulers' will on the officials. Emperor Taizu himself had passed a law banning eunuchs from working in the government, but he had violated his own rule, and so did all the other Ming emperors. Confucian scholar-officials tended to hate eunuchs and to fear their

During the Ming, some eunuchs working in the royal palace became wealthy enough to build or buy large estates with elegant reception halls. They typically lost power with the death of their masters, however, and their property fell into the hands of others, in this case a member of the Ming royal family.

potential influence over emperors. The conflict between the "inner palace" (eunuchs) and the "outer palace" (officials) was a frequent cause of problems in the Han, Tang, and Ming periods.

Yongle took a more expansive approach to foreign policy than his father, although compared with Khubilai Khan, his approach was still largely defensive. His own political base was in the north, and he built a new capital at Beijing (which means "northern capital"), near the site of the old Mongol capital of Dadu. To minimize conflict with the Mongols, he drew back his frontier guard units and stationed them within the Great Wall, which he rebuilt well to the south of the defense line of early times. Timur Leng died in 1405, just as he was planning an invasion of China, sparing the Ming a potentially serious problem. But hostile Mongol tribes posed new challenges to the security of the northern frontier.

In 1409 the emperor sent soldiers to the steppe to punish the Tatars for killing a Ming envoy. When the Chinese army was defeated, Yongle took personal charge of the four following expeditions. Although he was unable to capture a major Mongol leader, or put an end to the Mongol threat, he did manage to keep the Mongols on the other side of the Great Wall. By the early 15th century, trade through central Asia declined. This was in part because some of the oasis cities of Central Asia, important stops on the Silk Road, had not fully recovered from Timur Leng's wars of conquest. It was also because the Ming was never able to gain direct control over the steppe and the western region of central Asia. Caravans still traveled on the Silk Road, but the large-scale exchange of goods and ideas across the Asian continent was mostly a thing of the past.

Despite the hostilities to the north and the decline of the Silk Road trade, Ming China was secure and prosperous within its borders. The country's economy grew rapidly. Agriculture was the foundation of the economy, but cotton and silk cloth were produced by workers in factories, as well as by farm-women at home. Tea was grown, processed, and packaged both for domestic sale and for export. Ming porcelain with designs in cobalt blue on a pure white background was in demand throughout the world. With the relative decline of the Silk Road, trade over water routes increased.

THE VOYAGES OF THE TREASURE FLEETS

Perhaps to make up for his inability to dominate the steppe, the Emperor Yongle turned his attention to the lands south of China. He built a large imperial fleet to extend Ming influence overseas. From 1403 to 1406 he ordered shipyards in Nanjing and in five neighboring provinces to build or repair more than 1,600 ships, the largest of which were 440 feet long, five times the size of the ships that European explorers used a century later. The shipbuilders designed and built these ships using technology that was developed in the Song period. They had stern-post rudders, which were more efficient in steering than oars at the side of the boat, watertight compartments, and up to nine masts. The fleet included treasure ships (to bring rare goods back from foreign countries), troop ships, war ships (armed with cannons), horse-transport ships, supply ships, and water tankers.

During the 15th century, Ming rulers and officials organized farmers and workers to construct a series of long walls, later known in the West as the Great Wall. The wall across northern China kept ambitious Mongol leaders from raiding villages and seeking to restore their rule over China. Workers used large earthen bricks and cut stone blocks to strengthen earlier walls and fortify natural ridges to create a system that extended some 3,000 miles.

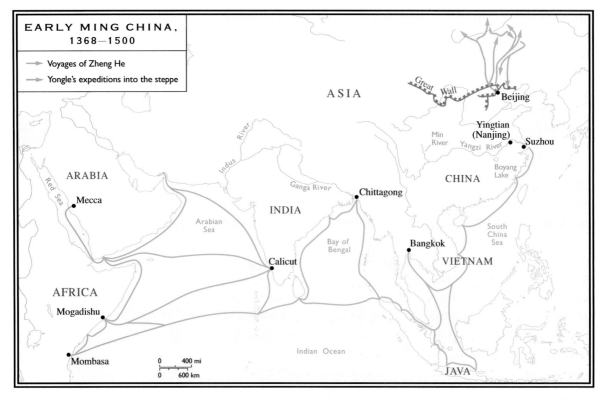

EARLY MING CHINA,
1368–1500

→ Voyages of Zheng He
→ Yongle's expeditions into the steppe

The emperor appointed a Muslim eunuch named Zheng He as chief admiral of the fleet. Zheng's ancestors were Central Asians who had moved to Yunnan, a province in China's far southwest. When the Ming army defeated the last Yuan loyalists in Yunnan in 1382, the Ming commander took the young Zheng He prisoner, had him made a eunuch, and gave him to Prince Zhu Di, the future Yongle emperor, as a servant. Zheng He proved to be brave, intelligent, and a natural leader; he served Zhu Di well as a military commander during the civil war in which Zhu Di won the throne. Though Zheng He did not have much experience at sea when he was appointed chief admiral, the emperor's faith in his abilities was justified. Zheng He turned out to be one of the greatest ocean explorers in world history.

From 1405 to 1421, Yongle authorized six expeditions to the South China Sea and the Indian Ocean that visited about three dozen states from Vietnam to East Africa. As the first expedition departed in 1405, bound for the west coast of India, the emperor publicly proclaimed: "Now all within the four seas are one family. . . . Let there be trade on the frontier to supply the country's needs and encourage distant people to come." The fleets, consisting of dozens of large ships and hundreds of smaller ones, were a clear demonstration of China's wealth and power, and the expeditions made a powerful impression on the states they visited. The main purpose of the voyages was to establish diplomatic relations with foreign countries and to engage in trade that was mutually beneficial. Admiral Zheng planned each new voyage carefully so he could revisit countries allied with China and explore new places. On his fifth voyage, which visited East Africa, Admiral Zheng brought back a giraffe that people took to be a *qilin,* a mythical animal that would appear only during the reign of an exceptionally good emperor.

By the 1420s the emperor became preoccupied with the expense of rebuilding the Forbidden City, as the imperial palace in Beijing was called, and by the troublesome northern frontier. For these reasons, perhaps, and because ocean voyages had already served their purpose, he became less enthusiastic about them. When Yongle died in 1424, on his way home from a war in Mongolia, his successor ordered that all voyages of the treasure ships be stopped. The Ming began to return to Taizu's policy of drawing back within its frontiers and avoiding unnecessary foreign conflicts.

However, in 1430 the new emperor, Xuanzong, authorized Zheng He to lead a seventh voyage to the Indian Ocean, intending "to instruct these countries to follow the

Although he returned with wonderful, precious things, what benefit was it to the state?

—Liu Daxia, vice president of the Ministry of War, commenting on Zheng He's treasure voyages in 1477, as reported by Gu Qiyuan in *Idle Talk with Guests,* 1617

When Yongle moved the Ming central government to Beijing (the northern capital), he established his court in what was called the Forbidden City. The Forbidden City was surrounded by a moat and a wall. Scholar-officials could enter the city through the south gate to take the palace examinations or to attend a royal audience, but the apartments to the north were reserved for the royal family and its attendants.

way of Heaven with reverence and to watch over their people so that all might enjoy the good fortune of lasting peace." Sensing that this might be his last voyage, Zheng wrote an epitaph, a funeral inscription, that was carved on stones at the mouths of the Yangzi and Min Rivers, where he assembled his final fleet. It read: "The great Ming dynasty, in unifying seas and continents, surpasses the Three Dynasties [the Xia, Shang, and Zhou of ancient times] and even goes beyond the Han and Tang." The seventh voyage, which lasted from 1431 to 1433, was the largest of all. It included 300 ships and 27,500 men, and it ventured all the way to East Africa. Zheng He, however, died during the voyage and was probably buried at sea.

With the death of the eunuch Admiral Zheng, officials who opposed eunuchs in positions of power and military expansion strongly urged the emperor to end ocean voyages once and for all. Already in 1430 the scholar Fan Ji had urged that the expeditions be stopped, saying that they were a distraction and that the Chinese should devote themselves to agriculture and education. A series of crop failures and famines in the 1430s made it easy for officials to say that spending money on eunuch enterprises was "wasteful." After the death of Emperor Xuanzong in 1435, Ming sea power quickly declined. By 1440, the fleet of the coastal province of Zhejiang had decreased from 700 ships to 350. Inland barges instead of coastal ships were used more and more to move goods from southern China to the north.

The Ming government continued to try to control ocean commerce. Officials severely punished merchants who conducted unlicensed overseas trade, and it was a capital offense to build ships of more than two masts. But the Ming state had a limited ability to restrict private trade. China continued to export large quantities of silk, tea, and porcelain in return for silver and local Southeast Asian products.

Yongle's favorite admiral, Zheng He, commanded seven fleets of hundreds of ships and sailed to Southeast Asia, India, the Middle East, and Africa. Like this ship model from the early 20th century, the Ming treasure ships had five or more masts and were equipped with stern-post rudders. Ming ships were more than 400 feet in length, five times the size of Columbus's Santa Maria, *which crossed the Atlantic six decades after Zheng He's voyages.*

This bowl is an example of the fine porcelain, produced at newly flourishing industrial towns in southeastern China, that made up a good share of Ming China's high-value exports to the rest of the world. Made of kraak ware, named after the Portugese ships (caracca) that brought such trade goods to Europe, the bowl features a cobalt blue underglaze as well as Buddhist emblems and a Latin inscription meaning "to the wise man nothing is new."

In the late 15th and 16th centuries, Westerners became interested in the cotton textiles of South Asia; the spices of Southeast Asia; and the silk, porcelain, and tea of East Asia, and European states began to send out their own armed expeditions to explore and trade. India and China's taste for gold and silver, which was needed to run their busy commercial economies, drew them into increasing trade with the West. This trade was mutually beneficial for two or even three more centuries before Europeans were finally able to take control of it, and turn it to their own greater advantage.

A Ming Dynasty Joke

FENG MENGLONG, "THE GOD OF THE ARCHERY TARGET HELPS WIN THE WAR," FROM THE EXPANDED TREASURY OF LAUGHS, 1574–1645

After Emperor Yongle died in 1420, the foreign policy of the Ming dynasty relied on payments and diplomacy, rather than on military power, to keep peace with various people who lived along China's frontiers. The Ming armed forces, which were used only defensively, grew weak and lacked training. The Ming Chinese, heirs to a long tradition of valuing the civil over the martial arts, a tradition reinforced by the reaction against the Mongols, did not respect military men very much. In his book The Expanded Treasury of Laughs, *the late Ming humorist Feng Menglong tells a joke about a general who couldn't shoot straight.*

A military officer engaged in a campaign was on the verge of being defeated, when suddenly a superhuman warrior joined his formation. Thus the officer ended up achieving a great victory instead. The officer bowed to the warrior and asked to know his name. "I am the spirit of the archery target," said the superhuman warrior. "What virtue does a humble general like me have that would induce you, O honored spirit, to trouble yourself to come to my aid? [asked the officer]" To which the spirit replied, "I was moved by the fact that, when you practiced on the archery range, you never once wounded me with an arrow."

GLOSSARY

ahimsa (uh-HIM-suh) Sanskrit word meaning "do no harm," an important concept in Indian religions, especially Jainism

bakufu (BAHK-oo-foo) Japanese word for the "tent government" of a shogun

bhakti (BUHK-tee) Sanskrit word meaning "devotion"; in Indian religion, the concept of devotion to a beloved god

Bodhisattva (bow-dih-SAHT-vuh) Sanskrit word meaning "awakened being," a fully enlightened being who postpones becoming a Buddha in order to help others attain salvation

bone rank Korean system of ranking members of the aristocracy

bonsai (BOHN-sai) Japanese word meaning "tray plant," a Zen-related pastime of raising miniature trees

Brahminism Ancient religion of India, from which Buddhism, Hinduism, and Jainism developed

Buddha Sanskrit word meaning "enlightened being," one who has escaped the cycle of rebirth by overcoming desire

Buddhism religion based on the teachings of Siddhartha Gautama, the Buddha

Bushido (BOO-shee-doh) Japanese word meaning the Way of the Warrior, a Zen-based code of warrior conduct

calligraphy beautiful writing, an important art form in several Asian cultures

cavalry horse troops, warriors mounted on horseback

concubine a secondary or junior wife

Confucianism philosophy based on the teachings of Kongzi (Confucius), influenced by other schools of thought such as Legalism; important in China, Korea, and Japan

daimyo (DAI-meeyoh) Japanese word meaning "great name," an aristocrat who rules a large territory and controls his own military forces

Dao (daow) Chinese word meaning the Way, the fundamental force of the universe underlying all things

Daoism philosophy and religion based on the concept of the Dao or Way

dharma Sanskrit word meaning "truth" and "duty," a fundamental concept in Hinduism, Buddhism, and Jainism

down-the-line trade trade in which goods travel long distances by changing hands several times

dynasty family that rules for two or more generations

eunuch neutered man, often employed in the inner quarters of a palace

filial piety respect and obedience a child owes to a parent; an important principle in Confucianism

Four Noble Truths basic teaching of Buddhism: all life is suffering, which comes from desire, which can be overcome by following the Noble Eightfold Path

Hinayana *see* Theravada

Hinduism Indian religion with many different variations, most of which stress personal devotion to one or more gods

Islam Arabic word meaning "submission" (to God); religion founded in Arabia by Muhammad in the seventh century CE

Jainism Indian religion stressing the concept of *ahimsa* ("doing no harm")

kamikaze (kah-mee-KAH-zay) Japanese word meaning "divine wind," used to describe the storms that helped repel Mongol invasions in the late 13th century

khan Turkish and Mongolian word meaning "leader," especially of a tribe or tribal confederation

Mahayana (mah-huh-YAH-nuh) Sanskrit word meaning the "Great Vehicle," a school of Buddhism that stresses achieving salvation through the grace of a Bodhisattva

mandala (MAHN-duh-luh) Sanskrit word meaning "circle"; a symbolic diagram representing various cosmic forces

Mandate of Heaven Chinese belief that heaven has granted the founder of a dynasty the right to rule because of his great virtue

mercenary soldier who fights because he is paid rather than because he has personal loyalty to a state

moksha (MOHK-shah) Sanskrit word meaning release from the cycle of reincarnation, a goal in Hinduism, Buddhism, and Jainism

mono no aware (mo-no no ah-wah-ray) Japanese phrase meaning "fragility of things," beauty which is more intense because it will not last

monsoon Arabic word meaning "seasonal winds," especially in the Indian Ocean and South China Sea

Muslim Arabic word meaning "one who submits" (to the will of God); a believer in Islam

Neo-Confucianism new and more spiritual form of Confucianism than the original teachings of Kongzi; created by Chinese scholars in the Song dynasty, partly in response to Buddhist and Daoist ideas

Noble Eightfold Path Buddhist means of overcoming desire: right views, intention, speech, action, livelihood, effort, mindfulness, and concentration

Noh Japanese word meaning "ability," Zen-influenced form of theater

oasis area of greenery in a desert made possible by a source of water

pagoda tall tower, usually as part of a Buddhist temple, used to hold sacred relics. *See also* stupa

pastoral nomads animal herders who migrate seasonally

prefecture an administrative unit in China made up of several counties

qilin (chee-lin) Chinese mythical animal that appears only during a period of exceptionally good government

Qur'an (kuh-RAHN or kuh-RAN) Arabic word meaning "recitation"; the sacred book of Islam

raja (RAH-jah) Sanskrit word meaning "king," the usual title of a ruler of India

regent person who exercises power and authority on behalf of a ruler, usually when the ruler is a child

samurai (SAM-uh-rai) Japanese word meaning "one who serves," a member of the warrior class in Japan

sari (SAH-ree) traditional one-piece wrapped dress worn by South Asian women

shah Persian word meaning "king"

shaman religious practitioner, especially in northern Asia, believed to be able to make contact with gods or spirits of the dead while in a state of trance

Shinto (SHIHN-tow) Japanese word meaning "Way of the gods," ancient religion of Japan

shogun (SHOW-guhn) Japanese word meaning "general," title of Japanese military rulers from 1185 to 1868

Son of Heaven title used by the rulers of China from the Zhou dynasty to 1911

steppe high, dry grasslands similar to a prairie

stupa domed building used to house holy relics as part of a Buddhist temple in Asia

sultan Arabic word meaning "ruler" or "king"

sutra (SOO-trah) Sanskrit word meaning "thread"; a sacred scripture of Buddhism believed to be the words of the Buddha

Tantra form of Buddhism that relies on sacred gestures, symbols, and rituals to represent the triumph of good over evil

Theravada (thehr-uh-VAH-duh) Sanskrit word meaning "teachings of the elders," one of the two main branches of Buddhism, sometimes called Hinayana or "Lesser Vehicle"

tribal confederation alliance of two or more tribes, usually under strong leadership to conduct offensive or defensive warfare

vizier (vih-ZEER) Arabic word meaning "helper," a minister or prime minister in the government of an Islamic state

water clock a device that uses a regulated flow of water to tell time

yugen (YEW-gehn) Japanese word meaning "mysteriousness," a quality of Noh theater and other Zen-related arts

Zen from the Chinese word *chan*, meaning "meditation"; school of Buddhism relying on meditation and discipline rather than texts and rituals to achieve enlightenment

Zoroastrianism ancient religion of Persia that sees the world as a struggle between good (symbolized by a sacred fire) and evil

TIMELINE

BCE

551
Kong Zhongni (Confucius) is born in China

about 550
Siddhartha Gautama (Buddha) is born in India

324–about 200 CE
Maurya Empire unites most of India

272–232
King Ashoka rules Maurya Empire in India

221
Qin Shi Huangdi unites China

206 BCE–220 CE
Han dynasty rules China

about 100
Trade on Silk Road begins

CE

about 320–500
Gupta Empire rules much of India

514–540
Kim Wonjong rules as king of Silla, Korea

552
Koreans introduce Buddhism into Japan

589
Yang Jian reunites China and founds Sui dynasty

604
Prince Shotoku of Japan issues 17-article constitution

about 610–647
King Harsha rules north India

618
Li Yuan founds Tang dynasty in China

629–642
Chinese monk Xuanzang travels to India

632–647
Queen Sondok rules kingdom of Silla in Korea

646
Taika reforms introduce Chinese-style government to Japan

690–705
Wu Zhao, female emperor, rules China

710
Japanese court moves to new capital at Nara; Nara period begins and lasts until 784

712
Muhammad ibn Qasim, Muslim sultan, conquers Sind in India

747–752
Great Buddha statue built at Nara, Japan

755–763
An Lushan leads rebellion against Tang dynasty in China

795
Japanese court moves to new capital, Heian-kyo; start of Heian period, which lasts until 1185

about 800
Buddhists build Temple of Borobudur on the island of Java

about 850
Chola Empire founded in south India

about 900
Hindu king builds temple of Prambanan on the island of Java

875–884
Rebel Huang Chao leads an uprising against Tang dynasty in China

907
End of Tang dynasty in China

918
Wang Kon founds Koryo dynasty and reunifies Korea

927
Yelü Abaoji founds Khitan Liao dynasty in northern China

960
Zhao Kuangyin founds Song dynasty in China, which lasts until 1279

997–1027
Fujiwara Michinaga is power behind the throne in Heian Japan

1004
Mahmud of Gazni conquers Panjab in India

about 1010
Murasaki Shikibu writes *The Tale of Genji* in Japan

1016–1045
Airlangga rules kingdom of Mataram in Indonesia

1038
Tangut people found kingdom in northwestern China

1115
Jurchen people found Jin dynasty in northern China, which lasts until 1234

1127
Song dynasty loses northern China and moves capital to Lin'an

1156–60
Civil war between Taira and Minamoto clans in Japan

about 1160
Temujin, who becomes Genghis Khan, born in Mongolia

1172–76
Popular rebellions against Koryo dynasty in Korea

1176
Ch'oe family seizes power in Koryo, Korea

1185
In Japan, Minamoto clan defeats Taira; Kamakura shogunate founded

1206
Qutb-ud-Din Aybak founds Delhi sultanate in India

1206
Genghis Khan confirmed as ruler of all Mongols

1220
Hojo clan controls Kamakura shogunate in Japan

1227
Genghis Khan dies

1229
Great Khan Ogodei extends Mongol Empire into Russia

1236
Raziya becomes first and only woman sultan of Delhi

1249
Mongke becomes great khan of the Mongols

1260
Khubilai named as great khan of the Mongols

1270
Koryo king accepts Mongol control over Korea

1274
Japanese repel first Mongol invasion

1275
Marco Polo arrives in China

1277–87
Mongols send military expedition to Southeast Asia

1279
Chola Empire ends in south India

1281
Japanese repel second Mongol invasion

1296
Ala-ud-din Khalji becomes sultan of Delhi

1313
Mongol rulers reinstate civil service examinations in China

1325
China and Japan resume diplomatic relations after 500 years; Zen influence grows in Japan

1325
Muhammad bin Tughluq becomes sultan of Delhi

1326
Brothers Harihara and Bukka Sangama found Kingdom of Vijayanagara in southern India

1333
Emperor Godaigo rebels against Kamakura shogunate in Japan; end of Kamakura period; Arab traveler Ibn Battuta becomes minister of justice for Tughluq sultanate in India

1336
Ashikaga Takauji founds Ashikaga shogunate in Japan, which lasts until 1573

1367–68
Khubilai Khan's Yuan dynasty gains controls of China, which lasts until 1367

1368
Zhu Yuanzhang founds Ming dynasty in China, which lasts until 1644

1392
General Yi Songgye founds Choson dynasty in Korea; it lasts until 1910

1398
Timur Leng invades India and sacks Delhi

1402
Zhu Di begins Yongle reign in China

1405
Chinese admiral Zheng He makes his first voyage to Indian Ocean; Timur Leng dies and his empire rapidly collapses

1414–50
King Sejong rules Choson dynasty in Korea, launching a golden age

1431–33
Admiral Zheng He makes his seventh and final voyage

1443
Scholars invent Korean script

1467–77
Onin War begins Warring States period in Japan

1573
Ashikaga shogunate collapses in Japan

1644
Ming dynasty ends in China

FURTHER READING

Entries with 👥 indicate primary source material.

ASIA

Fairbank, John King, Edwin O. Reischauer, and Albert M. Craig. *East Asia: Tradition and Transformation.* New York: Houghton Mifflin, 1990.

CHINA

Hansen, Valerie. *The Open Empire: A History of China to 1600.* New York: W. W. Norton, 2000.

Major, John S. *The Land and People of China.* New York: Lippincott, 1989.

Mote, Frederick W. *Imperial China, 900–1800.* Cambridge, Mass.: Harvard University Press, 1999.

Temple, Robert. *The Genius of China.* London: Prion, 1998.

INDIA

👥 Basham, A. L. *The Wonder That Was India.* 3rd ed. New York: Taplinger, 1968.

Henderson, Carol E. *Culture and Customs of India.* Westport, Conn.: Greenwood, 2002.

Keay, John. *India: A History.* New York: Grove, 2000.

Thapar, Romila. *Early India: From the Origins to A.D. 1300.* Berkeley: University of California Press, 2003.

JAPAN

Morris, Ivan I. *The World of the Shining Prince: Court Life in Ancient Japan.* New York: Knopf, 1964.

Nardo, Don. *Traditional Japan.* San Diego: Lucent, 1995.

Shelley, Rex, Teo Chuu Yong, and Russell Mok. *Japan.* 2nd ed. New York: Marshall Cavendish, 2002.

Varley, H. Paul. *Japanese Culture.* 4th ed. Honolulu: University of Hawaii Press, 2000.

KOREA

DuBois, Jill. *Korea.* 2nd ed. New York: Benchmark, 2005.

Lee Ki-baik. *A New History of Korea.* Translated by Edward W. Wagner with Edward J. Schultz. Cambridge, Mass.: Harvard Yenching Institute, 1984.

Solberg, S. E. *The Land and People of Korea.* New York: HarperColllins, 1991.

Stickler, John, and Soma Han. *Land of Morning Calm: Korean Culture Then and Now.* Fremont, Calif.: Shen's Books, 2003.

MONGOLIA AND CENTRAL ASIA

Greenblatt, Miriam. *Genghis Khan and the Mongol Empire.* New York: Marshall Cavendish, 2001.

👥 Kahn, Paul. *The Secret History of the Mongols.* San Francisco: North Point, 1984.

👥 Major, John S. *The Land and People of Mongolia.* New York: Lippincott, 1990.

Morgan, David. *The Mongols.* Oxford, England: Blackwell, 1990.

SOUTHEAST ASIA

Goodman, Jim. *Thailand.* New York: Benchmark, 2002.

Major, John S. *The Land and People of Malaysia and Brunei.* New York: HarperCollins, 1991.

Miruri, Gouri. *Indonesia.* New York: Marshall Cavendish, 1990.

Smith, Datus. *The Land and People of Indonesia.* New York: Lippincott, 1983.

ATLASES

Barraclough, Geoffrey, ed. *The Times Atlas of World History.* London: Times Books, 1978.

Blunden, Caroline, and Mark Elvin. *Cultural Atlas of China.* New York: Facts on File, 1998.

Bregel, Yuri, ed. *An Historical Atlas of Central Asia.* Boston: Brill, 2003.

Colcutt, Martin, Marius Jansen, and Isao Kumakura, eds. *Cultural Atlas of Japan.* New York: Checkmark, 1988.

Johnson, Gordon, ed. *Cultural Atlas of India: India, Pakistan, Nepal, Bhutan, Bangladesh, and Sri Lanka.* New York: Facts on File, 1996.

Khan, Aisha. *A Historical Atlas of India.* New York: Rosen Books, 2003.

O'Brien, Patrick K. ed. *Atlas of World History.* New York: Oxford University Press, 1999.

Pluvier, Jan M., ed. *Historical Atlas of South-East Asia.* Boston: Brill, 1995.

DICTIONARIES AND ENCYCLOPEDIAS

Bowring, Richard, and Peter Kornicki, eds. *The Cambridge Encyclopedia of Japan.* New York: Cambridge University Press, 1993.

Ch'oe-Wall, Yang-Hi. *Encyclopedia of Korea.* New York: Columbia University Press, 2000.

Embree, Ainslie T., ed. *Encyclopedia of Asian History.* 4 vols. New York: Scribners, 1988.

Higham, Charles F. W. *Encyclopedia of Ancient Asian Civilizations.* New York: Facts on File, 2004.

Hockings, Paul, ed. *Encyclopedia of World Cultures: East and Southeast Asia.* New York: Macmillan, 1993.

Hockings, Paul, ed. *Encyclopedia of World Cultures: South Asia.* New York: Macmillan, 1992.

Hook, Brian, and Denis Twitchett, eds. *The Cambridge Encyclopedia of China.* New York: Cambridge University Press, 1991.

Ooi, Keat, ed. *Southeast Asia: A Historical Encyclopedia, from Angkor Wat to East Timor.* New York: ABC-CLIO, 2004.

Robinson, Francis, ed. *The Cambridge Encyclopedia of India, Pakistan, Bangladesh, Sri Lanka, Nepal, Bhutan, and the Maldives.* New York: Cambridge University Press, 1989.

BIOGRAPHIES

Dramer, Kim. *Kublai Khan.* New York: Chelsea House, 1990.

Dunn, Ross E. *The Adventures of Ibn Battuta: A Muslim Traveller of the 14th Century.* Berkeley: University of California Press, 1990.

Hoobler, Dorothy and Thomas. *Chinese Portraits.* Austin, Tex.: Raintree Steck-Vaughn, 1993.

Lange, Brenda. *Genghis Khan.* New York: Chelsea House, 2003.

McDonald, Fiona. *Marco Polo: A Journey through China.* New York: Franklin Watts, 1998.

Ratchnevsky, Paul. *Genghis Khan: His Life and Legacy.* Oxford, England: Blackwell, 1991.

Rossabi, Morris. *Khubilai Khan: His Life and Times.* Berkeley: University of California Press, 1988.

Verma, H. N. *100 Great Indians through the Ages.* Campbell, Calif.: GIP Books, 1992.

Wepman, Dennis, et al. *Tamerlane.* New York: Chelsea House, 1987.

Wriggins, Sally Hovey. *Xuanzang: A Chinese Pilgrim on the Silk Road.* Boulder, Colo.: Westview, 1998.

PRIMARY SOURCE COLLECTIONS

[66] deBary, William Theodore, Irene Bloom, and Joseph Adler, eds. *Sources of Chinese Tradition.* 2nd ed. New York: Columbia University Press, 2000.

[66] deBary, William Theodore, Donald Keene, George Tanabe, and Paul Varley, eds. *Sources of Japanese Tradition.* 2nd ed. New York: Columbia University Press, 2002.

[66] Embrey, Ainslie, Stephen N. Hay, and William Theodore deBary, eds. *Sources of Indian Tradition.* 2nd ed. New York: Columbia University Press, 1988.

[66] Lee, Peter H., and William Theodore deBary, eds. *Sources of Korean Tradition.* New York: Columbia University Press, 1996.

ART

Craven, Roy C. *Indian Art.* Revised ed. New York: Thames & Hudson, 1997.

Girard-Geslan, Maud, et al. *Art of Southeast Asia.* New York: Harry N. Abrams, 1998.

Juliano, Annette L., and Judith A. Lerner, eds. *Monks and Merchants: Silk Road Treasures from Northwest China.* New York: Harry N. Abrams, 2001.

Kim, Chewon, and Lena Kim Lee. *Arts of Korea.* Tokyo: Kodansha, 1974.

Stanley-Baker, Joan. *Japanese Art.* Revised ed. New York: Thames & Hudson, 2000.

Sullivan, Michael. *The Arts of China.* 4th ed. Berkeley: University of California Press, 1999.

[66] Tucker, Jonathan. *The Silk Road: Art and History.* Chicago: Art Media Resources, 2003.

DAILY LIFE

Benn, Charles. *Daily Life in Traditional China: The Tang Dynasty.* Westport, Conn.: Greenwood, 2002.

Dunn, C. J. *Everyday Life in Traditional Japan.* Boston: Tuttle, 1969.

Gernet, Jacques. *Daily Life in China on the Eve of the Mongol Invasion, 1250–1276.* New York: Macmillan, 1962.

Taylor, Robert. *Life in Genghis Khan's Mongolia.* San Diego: Lucent, 2001.

FOLKTALES AND LITERATURE

Bosley, Keith, ed. *Poetry of Asia.* New York: Weatherhill, 1979.

[66] Carter, Steven D. *Traditional Japanese Poetry: An Anthology.* Stanford, Calif.: Stanford University Press, 1991.

Gilchrist, Cherry, and Nilesh Mistry. *Stories from the Silk Road.* Cambridge, Mass.: Barefoot Books, 1999.

Gray, J. E. B., and Rosamund Fowler. *Tales from India.* New York: Oxford University Press, 2001.

[66] Keene, Donald. *Anthology of Japanese Literature.* New York: Grove, 1955.

[66] Mair, Victor, ed. *The Columbia Anthology of Traditional Chinese Literature.* New York: Columbia University Press, 1994.

McAlpine, Helen, William McAlpine, and Rosamund Fowler. *Tales from Japan.* New York: Oxford University Press, 2002.

Souhami, Jessica, and Paul McAlinden. *Rama and the Demon King: An Ancient Tale from India.* New York: DK, 1997.

[66] Murasaki Shikibu. *The Tale of Genji.* Trans. Royall Tyler. New York: Viking, 2001.

[66] Owen, Stephen. *An Anthology of Chinese Literature: Beginnings to 1911.* New York: W. W. Norton, 1996.

van Buitenen, J. A. B. *Tales of Ancient India.* Chicago: University of Chicago Press, 1959.

Washburn, Katharine, and John S. Major, eds. *World Poetry: An Anthology of Verse from Antiquity to Our Time.* New York: W. W. Norton, 1998.

Watson, Burton. *The Columbia Book of Chinese Poetry.* New York: Columbia University Press, 1984.

Wu Cheng'en. *Monkey: A Folk Novel of China.* Trans. Arthur Waley. New York: Grove, 1994.

OCEAN TRADE AND VOYAGES

Chaudhuri, K. N. *Trade and Civilization in the Indian Ocean.* Cambridge, England: Cambridge University Press, 1985.

Levathes, Louise. *When China Ruled the Seas: The Treasure Fleet of the Dragon Throne, 1405–1433.* New York: Oxford University Press, 1996.

Mirsky, Jeannette. *The Great Chinese Travelers: An Anthology.* New York: Pantheon, 1964.

RELIGION

Ch'en, Kenneth. *Buddhism in China.* Princeton, N.J.: Princeton University Press, 1972.

Esposito, John L. *The Islamic World: Past and Present.* New York: Oxford University Press, 2004.

Kitagawa, Joseph. *Religion in Japanese History.* New York: Columbia University Press, 1966.

Miller, Barbara Stoler, trans. *The Bhagavad-Gita: Krishna's Counsel in Time of War.* New York: Bantam, 1986.

Thomson, Laurence G. *Chinese Religion: An Introduction.* Belmont, Calif.: Wadsworth, 1996.

Trainor, Kevin ed. *Buddhism: The Illustrated Guide.* New York: Oxford University Press, 2001.

Wilkinson, Philip, and Batul Salazar. *Eyewitness Islam.* New York: Dorling Kindersley, 2002.

Yao Xinzhong. *An Introduction to Confucianism.* Cambridge, England: Cambridge University Press, 2000.

SCIENCE

Beshore, George. *Science in Ancient China.* New York: Franklin Watts, 1998.

Beshore, George. *Science in Early Islamic Culture.* New York: Franklin Watts, 1998.

Williams, Suzanne, and Andrea Fong. *Made in China: Ideas and Inventions from Ancient China.* Berkeley, Calif.: Pacific View, 1997.

THE SILK ROAD

Major, John S. *Silk Road Encounters: Sourcebook.* New York: The Silk Road Project and the Asia Society, 2001.

Major, John S., and Stephen Fiesser. *The Silk Route: 7,000 Miles of History.* New York: Harper Trophy, 1996.

[66] Polo, Marco. *The Travels.* Trans. Sir Henry Yule. London: Everyman's Library, 1967.

Whitfield, Susan. *Life along the Silk Road.* Berkeley: University of California Press, 1999.

WARFARE

Gaskin, Carol. *Secrets of the Samurai.* New York: Avon, 1990.

Hall, Eleanor J. *Life among the Samurai.* San Diego: Lucent, 1999.

WEBSITES

ASIA

Ask Asia
www.AskAsia.org
Sponsored by the Asia Society, this site has information on Asian geography, history, arts, and politics, as well as a glossary of Asian terms.

CHINA

China Knowledge
www.chinaknowledge.de
"A universal guide for China studies," maintained by German scholars (but in English). It is a useful source of information on China with detailed coverage of Chinese history.

China Page
www.chinapage.com
This site about traditional Chinese culture is sponsored by an organization called China the Beautiful.

INDIA

India Nest
www.IndiaNest.com
A site designed for people of South Asian heritage as well as the general public; features information on all aspects of Indian culture.

JAPAN

Kids Web Japan
http://web-jpn.org/kidsweb/index.html
Designed especially for American students, this site has information on Japanese culture presented in a fun and lively way.

KOREA

Korea Overseas Information Service
www.korea.net
Sponsored by the government of South Korea, this site contains a lot of information on Korea, but more about the present day than historical subjects.

Korea Society
www.koreasociety.org
This site includes overviews of Korean history as well as links to general sites on Korea, news sources, and museums with Korean art collections.

MONGOLIA

Mongolia Society
www.indiana.edu/~mongsoc/mongolia.html
A good source of information on all aspects of Mongolian history, culture, and society.

RELIGION

Buddha Net
www.buddhanet.net
A site for all things relating to Buddhism, including information on Buddhist studies and an eBook library.

THE SILK ROAD

Silk Road
http://depts.washington.edu/uwch/silkroad/
The University of Washington runs this useful site on Silk Road–related subjects.

Silk Road Foundation
www.silk-road.com
This site has interesting information and links relating to Mongolia and the Silk Road.

Silk Road Project
www.silkroadproject.org/
Sponsored by the cellist Yo-Yo Ma's Silk Road Project, which is devoted to the spread of the arts along the Silk Road, this site covers Silk Road topics with a special emphasis on music.

INDEX

References to illustrations and their captions are indicated by page numbers in **bold**.

Abaoji, Yelü, 78–79
Acupuncture, 145
Afghanistan, 48, 52, 54, 98
Africa, 157, 159
Ahimsa, 25
Airlangga, 63–64
Alai Darwaza building, **105**
Ala-ud-din Khalji, 105–07
Arts, **82**, 87, **117**, **121**, 135–35
Ashikaga, Takauji, 131–32
Ashikaga shoguns, 132, 135
Ashoka, 26–27
Astronomy, 67–68, 145–46
Avelokitesvara, **143**
Avicenna, 58
Aybak, Qutb-ud-Din, 54, 102–04

Bai Juyi, 41
Bakufu, 126
Bamboo, **82**
Ban Gu, 60
Barani, Zia ud-Din, 106, 107
Beijing, 96, 154, **158**
Bhakti, 111
Bhoj of Parmara, 53
Bodhisattvas, 23, **24**, **30**, 35–36, **42**, **143**
Bone ranks, 66–67, 137
Borte, 92, 93
Brahminism, 20, 25, 26
Buddha, 20–**21**, **30**, **38**, **39**, **64**, **128**
Buddhism, 20–21, 23, 24, 26, 27, 28–29, **30**, 32–37, 40, 49–51, 59, 62–63, 66, 68, 69, 70, 85, 123, 127–29
Bukhara, 58, 97
Bushido, code of, 129
Byzantine Empire, 65
Byzantium, 38

Camels, **55**, 56
Canals, 116. *See also* Grand Canal
Caste, 26

Cathay, 116
Ceramics, Korean, **144**
Ch'oe family, 137, 138
Chang'an, 16, 33, 36, 71
Changchun (Qiu Chuji), 92
Chen dynasty, 32
Chengzong, 121
Chola, 51
Choson dynasty, 137, **139**–47
Choson T'aejo. *See* T'aejo
Christians, 47, 59
Clans, 93
Clock, water, 146
Clothing, 17–18, **97**, 103
Coins, **23**
Compass, 60, 83–84
Confucianism, 27–28, 32, 40–42, 69, 85–86, 88, 141–44, 151, 152
Confucius, **22**
Crowns, **67**
Currency. *See* Coins, Paper money

Dadu, 116, 150, 154
Daimyo, **124**, 126, 135
Daitokuji Temple, **133**
Daoism, 22, 29, 86
Delhi, 102, 104, 107–08
Delhi sultanate, 102–09, 110
Dharma, 21, 26
Diamond Sutra, **37**
Dogen, 132
Down-the-line trade, 57
Du Fu, 40
Dunhuang, **29**, 59

Eastern Expedition Field Headquarters, 138
Economy, 16–17, 154–55
Education, 35, 80–81, 150. *See also* Examination system
Equal field system, 35
Examination system, 28, 35, 70, 80–83, 117, 119, 121, 150

Families, **29**
Fan Ji, 159

Fan Kuan, 87
Fancheng, 116
Farming, 16–17, 35, **85**, **118**, 145
Fascination of Nature, The, **121**
Faxiang, **72**
Feng Menglong, 160
Fire powder, 84
Foot binding, 88–90
Forbidden City, **158**
Four Noble Truths, 21
Fujiwara family, 73, 75, 77, 124
Fujiwara Michinaga, 73, 76

Ganga River, 45
Gardens, Zen, **133**
Gautama, Siddhartha, 20–21
Gazni, 52
Genghis Khan, 91, **93**–99. *See also* Temujin
Godaigo, 131–32
Going Up the River on the Qingming Festival, 78, 86–87
Golden Horde, 99
Government, 22, 23, 27–28, 32, 69–70, 73, 77, 80–83, 117–19, 122, 139. *See also* Examination system, Confucianism
Grand Canal, 33, **34**, 116, 118
Great Assemblies, 93, 95, 99, 115
Great Wall, 23, **155**
Guanxu, 37
Gunpowder, 84
Guo Shoujing, 116
Guo Xi, 88
Gupta Empire, **25**, 27, 45

Hall of Worthies, 141, 145
Han dynasty, 23, 27–29, **30**, 36
Han Yü, 39
Hanfeizi, 23
Hangzhou, 83
Haniwa, **70**
Hanlin Academy, 123
Hanyang (Seoul), 140–41
Harp, **19**
Harsha Vardhana, 45–46
Heian period, 72–77

Heian-kyō, 72, 73, 74, 124
Hinayana, 23
Hindi language, 103
Hinduism, 25–26, 47, 51, 54,
    63–64, 102, 103, 108–09, 111
Ho'elun, 91, 92
Hojo clan, 126–27, 128
Hojo regency, 126, 131
Horyuji, 70
Huang Chao, 42

Ibn Battuta, Abu 'Abdallah, 62,
    107–08, 109
Ibn Sina, 58
Iltumish, 104
Indian Ocean, trade, 60–62, 156,
    157–59
Indonesia. See Java
Iryon, 67
Islam, 45, 47–48, 52–54, 64, 102

Jainism, 23–25, 26
Java, 62–64, 121
Jews, 47–48
Jin dynasty, 83, 94, 99, 96
Jingdezhen, 118–19
Jochi, 97, 99
Jurchen people, 83, 84, 94, 96, 118

Kabir, 111–12
Kaesong, 137, 140
Kafur Malik, 105–06
Kaifeng, 78, 79, 83, 86–87, 99
Kalidasa, 50
Kamakura, 124, 126
Kamakura period, 126–29
Kamikaze, 131
Karma, 20
Khanbaliq, 116
Khitan people, 78, 83, 96, 118
Khubilai Khan, 100, 113, 114–21,
    146
Khwarazm, 97
Ki no Tsurayuki, 77
Kim family, 137
Kim Wonjong, 66
Kiyomori, Taira, 124–25
Kong Zhongni, 21–22
Koryo, 136, 137–38, 142–43
Koryo dynasty, 69
Kuiji, 72
Kyoto, 72, 126, 131–32, 135

Land reform, 35, 139
Laozi, 22
Laws, 96, 101, 151
Li Bai, 40
Li Qingzhao, 88
Li Shimin (Tang Taizong), 34–35
Li Yuan, 34–35
Liao dynasty, 78–79, 83
Lin'an, 83, 86, 117
Liu Bingzhong, 115, 116
Liu Daxia, 157
Lotus Mahal temple, 110
Lotus Sutra, 24, 127, 128

Mahadeviyakka, 43–44
Mahavira, 23–25
Mahayana, 23, 24
Mahmud of Gazni, 52–53
Maitreya, 123, 149
Mandala, 51, 63
Mandate of Heaven, 33
Mataram, 63
Mathematics, 48
Maurya Empire, 25, 26–27
Maurya, Chandragupta, 26
Medicine, 58, 145
Meditation, 132
Meng Yuanlao, 86
Mengzi, 28
Merkit tribe, 93, 94
Minamoto clan, 124–25, 127
Minamoto no Yoshi'ie, 77
Minamoto Yoritomo, 125–26
Minamoto Yoshitsune, 125
Ming dynasty, 136, 140, 149–60
Ming Taizu. See Taizu
Moksha, 25
Mongke, 100
Mongol conquest, reasons for, 96–97
Mongol Empire, 91–101, 115,
    137–38
Mongolia, 91, 95
Mongols, 91–92, 94, 154
Mono no aware, 74
Monsoons, 61
Mosques, 53, 102
Muhammad, 47
Muhammad bin Tughluq, 107–08,
    109
Muhammad Ghori, 54, 102
Muhammad ibn Qasim, 47
Munjong, 146–47
Murasaki Shikibu, 75–77

Musical instruments, 17, 18, 19
Muslims, 47, 54, 102–04, 111
Muso Soseki, 131, 132

Naimans, 94–95, 97
Nakoso barrier, 77
Nalanda University, 49
Nanren, 118
Nara, 70–72
Narayana, 52
Neo-Confucianism, 86
Nepal, 20–21
Nichiren, 128–129
Noble Eightfold Path, 21
Noh drama, 134–35
Nomads, 93, 96–97
Northern Zhou dynasty, 32

Observatories, 67, 145–46
Ocean trade, 59–62, 83, 156–59
Ogodei, 99, 100, 101
Onin War, 135
Otrar, 97

Paekche, 68
Pala dynasty, 49
Panjab, 52, 54
Paper, 57–58
Paper money, 116
Paris, Matthew, 99
People of the Book, 47
Persia, 38
Persian language, 103
Phagspa, 120
Poetry, 40, 41, 43, 47, 111–12, 147
Polo (game), 103
Polo, Maffeo, 113–14
Polo, Marco, 113–15, 119, 122
Polo, Nicolo, 113–14
Porcelain, 60, 86, 118–19, 154–55,
    160
Printing, 36, 37, 140, 141
Pure Land, 35, 127–28

Qilin, 157
Qin dynasty, 22–23, 33
Qin Shi Huangdi, 22–23
Qin, 17
Qiu Chuji (Changchun), 92, 98
Quran, 58

Rashid al-Din, 101, 116
Raziya, 104–05

Renzong, 121–23
Roman Empire, and trade, 60

Sailendra, 62–63
Samarkand, 97, 111
Samurai, **124**, 126, **129**
Sanskrit, 50
Scholar-officials, 35, 80, 82, 83, 117, 119, 121, 153–54
Sei Shonagon, 74
Sejong, 141–46
Shaikh Hamadani, 110
Shamans, 92
Shangdu, 116
Shingon (True Word), 127, **128**
Shinkei, 135
Shinran, 128
Shinto, 69
Shipping routes, 59–62
Ships, **61**, 83, 155, **159**
Shiva, 26, 43, **44**, 51, **52**
Shoguns, 125, 132, 135
Shotoku, prince, 69–70, **71**
Siddartha. *See* Gautama, Siddartha
Silk, 16–17, 28, **57**
Silk Road, 27, 28, 37, 38, 40, 55, 56–59, **59**, 65, 113, 146, 154
Silla, 66–69
Sind, 47, 48
Sirj, Minhaju-s, 104–05
Slaves, 102, 142–43
Son of Heaven, 31
Sondok, 67
Song dynasty, 79–90. *See also* Southern Song
Song Renzong, **81**
South Asia, geography of, 44–45
Southern Song, 83–90, 116–17
Spinning wheel, 107
Stupa, **49**
Su Dongpo, 82
Su Shi, 82
Sui dynasty, **31**–34
Sui Wendi, **32**–33
Sui Yangdi, 33, **34**
Suicide, ritual, 125
Suiko, 69
Sundial, **146**
Sutras, 24, 36, **37**
Suzhou, 149

T'aejo, 139–41. *See also* Yi Songgye
T'aejong, 141

Taika reforms, 70, 73
Tairo clan, 124–25, **127**
Taizong. *See* Tang Taizong
Taizu, 150–52, 153. *See also* Zhu Yuanzhang
Tale of Genji, The (Murasaki), 75–77
Tamerlane. *See* Timur Leng
Tang dynasty, 16–19, **31**, 34–42, 65
Tang Taizong, **35**, 38, 39, 67
Tang Xuanzong, 16, 39–40, **41**
Tangut people, 80
Tantra, 49–51
Tatars, 92, 94
Taxes, 99–100
Tea, 36–37, 133–34
Temples, **44**, 51, 62–63, **64**, 70, 72, 73, 102, 106, **110**, **112**, 132–33, **136**
Temujin, 91–93. *See also* Genghis Khan
Tendai, 127
Theravada, 23
Three Teachings, 115
Three Treasures of Buddhism, 69
Tibet, 49
Timur Leng, 110–11, 154
Timur the Lame. *See* Timur Leng
Tongman, 67
Trade, 27, **56**, 97, 138, 157, 159–60. *See also* Shipping routes, Silk Road, Ocean trade
Travel pass, Yuan, **113**, **123**
Travels (Polo, Marco), **113**, 114, 115, 122
Tribal society, 93–94
Tughluq, 107

Uighurs, 95, 96

Vairocana, 72
Vajra, 128
Vijayanagara, **106**, 108–09
Vishnu, 26, 64

Wang Anshi, 80
Wang family, 138
Wang Kon, 68–69, 137
Wang Wei, 18, 40
Warfare, 28, 37–38, **94**, **95**, 119, **127**
Warring States period, 135
Warriors, **68**, **70**, 77, **98**. *See also* Samurai

Water clock, 146
Way of the Warrior, 129
Weapons, 95, **98**
Wen Tong, 82
White Lotus sect, 123, 149
Women, 38–39, 67, 74–77, 87–90, 104–05, 135, 144, **151**
Wongwang, 68
Wonjong, 138
Writing, 71–72, 74, 96, 144–45
Wu Zhao, 38–39
Wu, 27–28, 55–56

Xi'an, 23
Xiangyang, 116
Xuanzang, 36, 46, 49, 55
Xuanzong, 157, 159

Yakut, 104
Yang Guifei, 39–40, **41**
Yang Jian, 31–33
Yasa, 101
Ye Xiaoluan, 90
Yelü Chucai, 99–100
Yi family, 137
Yi Songgye, 136–37, 139–40. *See also* T'aejo
Yingtian (Nanjing), 150
Yongle, 152–57
Yoritomo. *See* Minamoto Yoritomo
Yoshida Kenko, 130
Yoshitsune. *See* Minamoto Yoshitsune
Yū Renzhong, 87
Yuan dynasty, 113–23, 149, 150
Yugen, 135
Yusuf Has Hajip, 57

Zeami, 135
Zen, 129, 130
Zen arts, 132–35
Zhang Qian, 28, 56
Zhang Zeduan, 86
Zhao Kuangyin, 79
Zhao Mengfu, 121–23
Zheng He, 156–59
Zhongdu (Beijing), 96
Zhou dynasty, 39
Zhu Di, 152. *See also* Yongle, 156
Zhu Xi, 85–86
Zhu Yuanzhang. 148–**50**. *See also* Taizu
Zoroastrians, 47–48

TEXT AND PICTURE CREDITS

TEXT CREDITS

p. 23: *Hanfeizi,* in William Theodore DeBary, ed., Burton Watson, and Wing-tsit Chan. *Sources of Chinese Tradition* (New York: Columbia University Press, 1959), 145–46.

p. 24: Hurvitz, Leon, trans., *The Lotus Sutra,* in Victor Mair, ed., *The Columbia Anthology of Traditional Chinese Literature* (New York: Columbia University Press, 1994), 83.

p. 27: The Dhamma of Ashoka.

http://peaceworld.freeservers.com/140ASHOKA.htm

p. 28: Major, John S., trans.,*Mengzi* 1:1.

p. 36: Reischauer, E. O., *Ennin's Diary* (Cambridge, Mass.: Harvard University Press, 1955), 148–49.

p. 39: Han Yü, "Memorial on the Bone of the Buddha," in DeBary, Watson, and Chan., eds., *Sources of Chinese Tradition,* 428.

p. 40: Li Bai (Li Bo), "Fighting South of the Wall, No. 2," trans. Elling O. Eide, in Katherine Washburn and John S. Major, eds., *World Poetry* (New York: Norton, 1998), 244.

p. 41: Bai Juyi, "Song of Unending Sorrow," trans. John S. Major.

p. 47: Anon., "Eight Anthologies," trans. A. L. Basham in *The Wonder That Was India,* (New York: Taplinger, 1968), 469.

p. 49: Adapted from Xuanzhang, *Journey to the West,* trans. Samuel Beal, 1884, in Sally Hovey Wriggins, *Xuanzang: A Chinese Pilgrim on the Silk Road* (Boulder, Colo,: Westview, 1998), 125–26.

p. 50: Kalidasa, "The Birth of the War God," trans. A. L. Basham in *The Wonder That Was India* (New York: Taplinger, 1968), 423–24.

p. 52: Narayana, *Hitopadesa,* trans. A. L. Basham in *The Wonder That Was India,* 454.

p. 57: Adapted from Yusuf Has Hajip, "The Knowledge Befitting a Ruler," in Owen Lattimore, *The Pivot of Asia: Sinkiang and the Inner Asian Frontiers of China and Russia* (Boston: Little, Brown, 1950), quoted in Jonathan Tucker, *The Silk Road: Art and History* (London and Chicago: Art Media Resources, 2003), 166.

p. 60: Adapted from Hirth, Friedrich, and W. W. Rockhill, ed. and trans., *Chau Ju-kua: His Work on the Chinese and Arab Trade in the Twelfth and Thirteenth Centuries, Entitled Chu-fan-chi* (Imperial Academy of Sciences: St. Petersburg and Tokyo, 1914), 156.

p. 62: Ibn Battuta in Sir Henry Yule, *Cathay and the Way Thither,* vol. 1 ([The Hakluyt Society: London, 1866), 94.

p. 65: Adapted from *Jiu Tang shu* trans. Friedrich Hirth in, *China and the Roman Orient: Researches into their Ancient and Mediaeval Relations as Represented in Old Chinese Records* (Kelly and Walsh: Shanghai & Hong Kong, 1885).

p. 68: *Haedong kosung chon,* in Lee and deBary, eds. *Sources of Korean Tradition,* 44–46.

p. 70: Ryusaku Tsunoda, William Theodore de Bary, and Donald Keene, *Sources of Japanese Tradition* (New York: Columbia University Press, 1958), 50–53.

p. 74: Sei Shonagon, *The Pillow Book,* trans. Ivan Morris (New York: Columbia University Press, 1991), 78.

p. 76: Murasaki Shikibu, *The Tale of Genji,* vol. 1, trans. Royall Tyler (New York: Viking, 2001), 6–17.

p. 77: Ki no Tsurayuki, "Spring," trans., Stephen D. Carter in *Traditional Japanese Poetry: An Anthology* (Stanford, Calif.: Stanford University Press, 1991), 104.

p. 80: Adapted from Wang Anshi, "Memorial to Emperor Renzong," trans. de Bary, Watson, and Chan, *Sources of Chinese Tradition,* 470.

p. 82: Adapted from Su Shi, "An Account of Wen Tong's Paintings of the Slanted Bamboo of Yun-dang Valley," in Stephen Owen, ed. and trans., *An Anthology of Chinese Literature: Beginnings to 1911* (New York: W.W. Norton, 1996), 642.

p. 86: Meng Yuanlao, trans. by Michael Freeman, "Sung," in K. C. Chang, ed., *Food in Chinese Culture* (New Haven, Conn.: Yale University Press, 1977), 161.

p. 88: Guo Xi, "Essay on Landscape Painting," in Wen Fong, *Summer Mountains* (New York: Metropolitan Museum of Art, 1975), n.p.

p. 92: Mirsky, Jeannette, *The Great Chinese Travelers: An Anthology* (New York: Pantheon, 1964), 128.

p. 96: Mirsky, *The Great Chinese Travelers,* 128.

p. 99: Giles, J. A., trans., *Matthew Paris's English History,* vol. 1 (Henry G. Bohn: London, 1852), 312–23.

p. 101: Rashid al-Din, *The Successors of Genghis Khan,* trans. John Andrew Boyle (New York: Columbia University Press, 1971), paraphrased in John S. Major, *The Land and People of Mongolia* (New York: Lippincott, 1990), 85.

p. 108: Ibn Battuta *Travels* in Sir Henry Yule, *Cathay and the Way Thither,* vol. 4 (London: The Haklyut Society, 1915), 114.

p. 109: Adapted from Ibn Battuta, *The Rehla of Ibn Battuta,* trans. Mahdi Husain (Baroda, India: Oriental Institute, 1976), 55.

p. 110: Hamadani, Shaikh, *The Treasuries of Kings,* in Ainslie Embrey, Stephen N. Hay, and William Theodore deBary, eds., *Sources of Indian Tradition,* 2nd ed., vol. 1 (New York: Columbia University Press, 1988), 412.

p. 120: Franke, Herbert, *From Tribal Chieftain to Universal Emperor and God: The Legitimation of the Yuan Dynasty* (Munich: Bavarian Academy of Science, 1978), quoted in Morris Rossabi, *Khubilai Khan: His Life and Times* (Berkeley: University of California Press, 1988), 144.

p. 122: Polo, Marco, *The Travels,* trans. Sir Henry Yule, (London: Everyman's Library, 1967), 207–8, 211–12.

p. 123: Li Jiannong (1957), in Frederick W. Mote, "China under Mongol Domination, 1234–1367," unpublished manuscript, n.d., about 43.

p. 129: Kamo no Chomei, *An Account of My Hut,* trans. Keene, *Anthology of Japanese Literature,* 206.

p. 130: Yoshida Kenko, *Essays in Idleness,* trans. Donald Keene, *Anthology of Japanese Literature* (New York: Grove, 1955), 233, 238.

p. 131: Muso Soseki, *Taisho daizokyo,* trans. Tsunoda and deBary, *Sources of Japanese Tradition,* 260.

p. 132: Muso Soseki, untitled poem in Carter, ed. and trans., *Traditional Japanese Poetry,* 269.

p. 135: Shinkei, untitled poem, in Carter, ed. and trans., *Traditional Japanese Poetry,* 291.

p. 142–43: Adapted from *Koryo sa* (History of the Koryo dynasty), in Lee and deBary, eds., *Sources of Korean Tradition,* (New York: Columbia University Press, 1996), 200.

p. 147: Kyunyo, Master, trans. Peter H. Lee, in Keith Bosley, ed., *Poetry of Asia* (New York: Weatherhill, 1979), 76.

p. 157: Gu Qiyuan, *Kezuo zhui yu* (Idle talk with guests), in Louise Levathes, *When China Ruled the Seas: The Treasure Fleet of the Dragon Throne, 1405–1433* (New York: Oxford University Press, 1996), 180.

p. 160: Feng Menglong, "The God of the Archery Target Helps Win the War," trans. in Victor Mair, ed., *The Columbia Anthology of Classical Chinese Literature* (New York: Columbia University Press, 1994), 662–63.

PICTURE CREDITS

ROGER V. DES FORGES is professor of history at the University at Buffalo. He holds a Ph.D. in Chinese history from Yale University. He has written extensively on Chinese history, including two books, *Cultural Centrality and Political Change in Chinese History: Northeast Henan in the Fall of the Ming* and *Hsi-liang and the Chinese National Revolution*. Professor Des Forges is co-editor, with Luo Ning and Wu Yen-bo, of *Chinese Democracy and the Crisis of 1989: Chinese and American Reflections*.

JOHN S. MAJOR is a senior lecturer at the Teach China Program of the China Institute and was associate professor of history at Dartmouth College. He received his M.A. and Ph.D. from Harvard University in history and East Asian languages. Major is the author and editor of numerous books and articles, including *Myth and Symbol in Chinese Tradition* and *Heaven and Earth in Early Han Thought*. He has also written books for young adults, including *The Land and People of China, The Silk Route: 7,000 Miles of History,* and *Caravan to America: Living Arts of the Silk Road*.

BONNIE G. SMITH is Board of Governors Professor of History at Rutgers University. She has edited a series for teachers on Women's and Gender History in Global Perspective for the American Historical Association and has served as chair of the test development committee for the Advanced Placement examination in European history. Professor Smith is the author of many books on European, comparative, and women's history, among them *Confessions of a Concierge* and *Imperialism: A History in Documents*. She is co-author of *The Making of the West: Peoples and Cultures,* editor in chief of the forthcoming Oxford encyclopedia on women in world history, and general editor of an Oxford world history series for high school students and general readers.